SCHOOL CLIMATE IMPROVEMENT: A CHALLENGE TO THE SCHOOL ADMINISTRATOR

Robert S. Fox, Chairman
Herbert E. Boies
Edward Brainard
Edward Fletcher
James S. Huge
Cecelia L. Martin
William Maynard
James Monasmith
James Olivero
Richard Schmuck
Thomas A. Shaheen
William H. Stegeman

About the Authors

Dr. Robert S. Fox is Director, ERIC Clearinghouse for Social Studies/Social Sciences Education, Boulder, Colorado, and Professor (On-Leave), University of Michigan

Herbert E. Boies is Principal, Viewlands Elementary School, Seattle, Washington, Public Schools

Dr. Edward Brainard is President, CFK Ltd., Englewood, Colorado

Edward Fletcher is Director, Research and Development, San Diego, California, City Schools

James S. Huge is Principal, Lincoln East High School, Lincoln, Nebraska, Public Schools

Cecelia J. Logan is Executive Assistant, CFK Ltd., Englewood, Colorado

William Maynard is Principal, Cleveland High School, Seattle, Washington, Public Schools

Dr. James Monasmith is Principal, Colville High School, Colville, Washington, Public Schools

Dr. James L. Olivero is Executive Director, Nueva Day School and Learning Center, Hillsborough, California

Dr. Richard Schmuck is Professor of Education, Center for Advanced Study of Educational Administration, University of Oregon, Eugene

Dr. Thomas A. Shaheen is Former Superintendent, San Francisco, California, Unified School District

Dr. William H. Stegeman is Deputy Superintendent, School Operations, San Diego, California, City Schools

Acknowledgements

This Occasional Paper uses many of the concepts of an earlier CFK Ltd. publication, *The Principal as the School's Climate Leader: A New Role for the Principalship,* by these CFK Ltd. Associates: Charles F. Kettering II, Robert S. Fox (Chairman), Edward Brainard, George Carnie, William Georgiades, Eugene R. Howard, and James L. Olivero.

In the first six months of 1973, about 200 school administrators involved in school climate improvement endeavors throughout the nation provided ideas and suggestions to earlier drafts of this paper. The content of this document is directly reflective of their efforts.

About CFK Ltd.

Founded by the late Charles F. Kettering II in 1967, CFK Ltd. is a Denver-based philanthropic foundation dedicated to improving administrative leadership and the learning climate of elementary and secondary schools.

Because the foundation exists to be of service to public education, all CFK Ltd. programs are determined and developed by educators. CFK Ltd. has appointed fifty-seven public school and university educators throughout the nation as Associates. They assist in developing the foundation's character, policies, and programs, and most direct CFK Ltd. related programs within their school systems. CFK Ltd. programs pertain to assisting school systems in:

—Developing individualized continuing education programs for their school administrators

—Developing learning programs for principals and other administrators so that they might serve as climate leaders within their schools and/or school systems

—Using the results of the above endeavors on a non-grant basis.

CFK Ltd. also sponsors the Annual Gallup Poll on "The Public's Attitudes Toward the Public Schools," which appears yearly in the *Phi Delta Kappan.*

The CFK Ltd. Board of Directors are:

—Dr. B. Frank Brown, Division Director, Information and Services, Institute for Development of Educational Activities (I/D/E/A), Melbourne, Florida

—Senator George L. Brown, Executive Director, Metro Denver Urban Coalition, and Member, Colorado State Senate, Denver, Colorado

—Jean S. Kettering, Chairwoman of the Board, CFK Ltd., Englewood, Colorado

—Leo C. McKenna, Vice President, Dominick & Dominick, Inc., New York, New York

TABLE OF CONTENTS

Preface

Climate: the trend of fundamental concepts and attitudes pervading a community, nation or era, as, intellectual climate.[1]

Providing Leadership for School Climate Improvement

In growing numbers, educators are concerned with developing a humane school climate. This book is for those educational leaders—principals, superintendents, assistant superintendents, and other school administrators—who want to take action to improve the school climate. It describes how to provide leadership for developing lasting and significant improvements in school climate. It also shows the growing necessity for a positive and humane school environment and reasons why the school's climate is crucial to its success.

At the outset, the school's climate is described in terms of 1) goals for the school's learning programs, 2) factors that comprise climate and determine its quality, 3) elements of a school's operation that contribute to a positive climate, 4) basic human needs that any school must address if it is to be a viable educational institution, and 5) goals for an effective staff development program.

Additionally, the book outlines how to take the first and most significant step toward climate improvement, which is to assess and analyze the climate within a school or school system. Such a process helps the educator determine concerns and

ix

needs, and, by establishing priorities, helps administrators, faculty, students, and parents to resist the bandwagon approach to school improvement and to do more than merely subscribe to the latest and most fashionable panaceas.

The major how-to-do-it contents of this book will deal with:

Procedures for developing the healthy climate needed by the school to support positive student growth

Defining school climate in practical language so the school can assess its quality

Avoiding the too-frequent tendency to leave school climate improvement to chance

Charting the administrator's responsibility in assessing climate and initiating action to improve leadership.

While the examples here deal largely with climate concerns as they pertain to individual elementary and secondary schools, it is not implied that only they need be concerned with the wholesomeness of their climate. The elements of a positive climate are equally applicable to school districts. Further, the authors believe they are applicable to the climate of the superintendency and the operating divisions of a school system, such as those dealing with curriculum development and instruction, maintenance and custodial services, finance, accounting and purchasing, personnel, research and development, and transportation. At least one university president believes that with minor adaptations, the concepts that follow offer guidance to improving key elements of university climate that traditionally have been overlooked. Thus, this book can be of value to leaders in all these categories as well as to principals.

How To Use This Book

School climate improvement is a challenging responsibility, and the options for the task spread across a wide range. This book describes some options and tells how to begin exercising them. The authors do not expect school administrators and faculties will be in a position to improve all climate aspects simultaneously. No doubt the administrator will wish to examine his own values and motivation before deciding what he wants to do to provide leadership for climate improvement.

A first step is gaining a new understanding of school climate and its components. We encourage study of Chapter I, "The Climate of the School." This part describes climate in practical terms and offers a brief climate assessment instrument the administrator can use to record his impressions of his school's climate.

A second step is examining the potential role of the school administrator in improving school climate. This is described in Chapter II, "Improving the School's Climate: A Challenge to the School Administrator." Here the administrator's potential role is weighed against his concept of it and against his strengths and deficiencies.

A third step concerns providing leadership for the conduct of large- and small-scale climate improvement projects. The subsequent parts provide actual processes and programs that can be used to assess climate, plan projects, and improve administrative abilities.

A Checklist

Use this checklist to determine the extent to which you believe it is feasible to use the wide range of resources and options offered here.

_____ To gain new understanding of school climate (See Chapter I.)

_____ To obtain an overview of the role of the school administrator in improving climate (See Chapters II and VIII.)

_____ To administer the CFK Ltd. School Climate Profile instrument to discover potential strengths and weaknesses of school climate (See Chapter V.)

_____ To obtain information and expertise in providing leadership for organizing school climate improvement projects (See Chapters III, IV, VI, and IX.)

_____ To conduct school climate improvement projects (See Chapters III and IV.)

(At the conclusion of Chapter I, you will again be referred to this checklist.)

CHAPTER I

The Climate of the School

Introduction

A positive school climate is both a means and an end. A good climate makes it possible to work productively toward important goals, such as academic learning, social development, and curriculum improvement.

It also makes school a good place to be, a satisfying and meaningful situation in which both adults and youth care to spend a substantial portion of their time.

What factors comprise a humane climate? How can people in a school insure that it has a wholesome learning climate? What guidelines can be developed to serve as a measure of the humaneness of a school's climate? These are the essential questions addressed in this book.

Usual writings on the characteristics of a good school's program describe the nature of the curriculum and the instructional program. That is, they describe 1) desirable classroom teaching-learning strategies and conditions, and 2) sets of courses and experiences to be offered students within each area of the curricular and extracurricular programs. This book goes beyond these concerns. It describes in concrete terms facets of the school's climate as they relate to school climate goals; how to assess climate; program, process, and material contributions necessary in a healthy climate; desirable relationships among educators, students, and others comprising the school community; and the leadership responsibilities of school administrators serving as climate leaders.

Importance of School Climate

During the past decade, great strides have been made in strengthening the American school system. Many new and architecturally inviting school buildings have been built in an effort to keep pace with the rapid increase in the population. New developments and major advances have occurred in program organization—scheduling alternatives, individualized instructional systems, varied approaches to staff utilization, multiple grouping arrangements, and a veritable explosion of multimedia instructional materials. Exciting new curriculum materials have emerged in mathematics, science, English, and the social sciences. Program management techniques such as the Planning-Programming-Budgeting System (PPBS), and behavioral objectives, accountability, and National Assessment programs have become available to help sharpen the focus of educational programs and support the evaluation of their effects.

Despite these strides, we have not totally succeeded in creating the kind of schools we would like to have; we are not achieving the potential we envision. Perennial problems and concerns about schools remain.

In the following list of problems, are any characteristic of your school? Check those which concern you or your faculty, students, or parents. Space is provided at the end of the list to add other problems encountered at your school.

___ High student absenteeism

___ High frequency of student discipline problems

___ Weak student government

___ Student cliques

___ High faculty absenteeism

___ Negative discussion in faculty lounges

___ Crowded conditions

___ "Lost" feeling of students because the school is too large

____ Vandalism

____ Student unrest

____ Poor school spirit

____ Poor community image of the school

____ Faculty cliques

____ Property theft from lockers

____ High student dropout rate

____ Underachieving students

____ Low staff morale

____ Passive students

____ Faculty apathy

____ Supplies and equipment unavailable when needed

____ Students carrying guns, knives, and other weapons

____ Poor image of the school by staff

____ Dislike of students by faculty members

____ Feeling among students that school has little purpose

____ High incidence of suspensions and expulsions

____

____

____

Most of these problems demand direct attention, and an alert administrator recognizes the need to correct the dysfunctional programs and processes that seem causal to the negative conditions, attitudes and behavior listed above.

Actually, such problems are symptoms of deeper climate concerns. They are the tips of icebergs, indicators of the inadequacy of a school's programs for dealing with the human needs of students, faculty, and, perhaps, administrators; they are, in fact, often effects rather than causes. Parenthetically, it could be said that if schools continue to perpetuate an anti-humane climate in which apathy, failure, punishment, and inadequate success in achieving the curriculum are characteristic, they may guarantee their own demise, and ultimately that of the American social system.

Goals of the Humane School Climate

It is easy to talk about a humane school, and to describe such an environment in glowing terms. But in reality, what is a truly humane school? What does a good climate look like? What are the characteristics of such a school's learning activities? What instructional conditions must exist? How can a school organization maintain efficiency and accountability in its learning program and still be centrally concerned with people? Can a school have trust and effective communication between administrators and teachers, between teachers and students and parents, and still retain respect for individuality and diverse value positions?

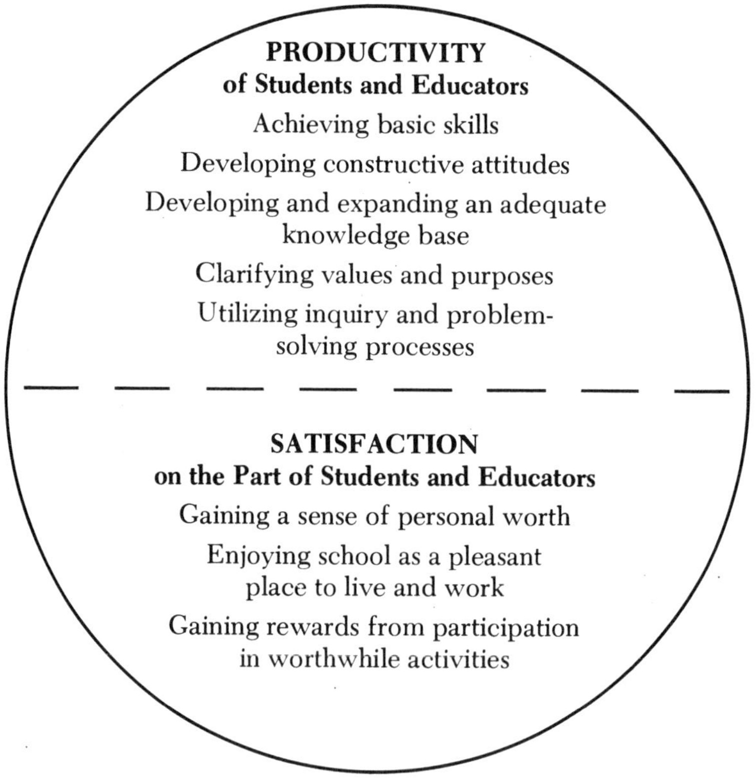

PRODUCTIVITY
of Students and Educators
Achieving basic skills
Developing constructive attitudes
Developing and expanding an adequate knowledge base
Clarifying values and purposes
Utilizing inquiry and problem-solving processes

SATISFACTION
on the Part of Students and Educators
Gaining a sense of personal worth
Enjoying school as a pleasant place to live and work
Gaining rewards from participation in worthwhile activities

Figure 1-1
SCHOOL CLIMATE GOALS

The authors believe it can. Contained in the answer are the two following goals of the humane school climate:

To provide throughout the school a wholesome, stimulating, and *productive* learning environment conducive to academic achievement and personal growth of youth at different levels of development

To provide a pleasant and *satisfying* school situation within which young people can live and work.

These primary goals focus on the young people for whom schools exist. A corollary is provision of a stimulating and productive environment for the adults of the school community —the faculty, principal, other staff members, and parents.

To summarize, these goals or outgrowths of a school climate can best be characterized as *productivity* and *satisfaction*. One without the other is insufficient. Figure 1-1 illustrates the goals.

Emergence of School Climate Awareness

More than fifty years ago, in 1918, the Commission on the Reorganization of Secondary Education articulated the Cardinal Principles of Secondary Education as health, command of fundamental processes, vocational efficiency, good citizenship, worthy home membership, worthy use of leisure time, and ethical character.[2] More recently, in 1938, the Educational Policies Commission of the National Education Association outlined the purposes of education in the American democracy for the everyday life pattern of an educated citizen. These were described as the objectives of self-realization, human relationship, economic efficiency, and civic responsibility.[3]

Using public opinion research processes, in 1973, the National Commission on the Reform of Secondary Education, chaired by B. Frank Brown, developed thirteen learner-centered goals for secondary education. They are:

Content goals

Achievement of communication skills

Achievement of computational skills

Attainment of proficiency in critical and objective thinking

Acquisition of occupational competence

Clear perception of nature and environment

Development of economic understanding

Acceptance of responsibility for citizenship

Process goals

Knowledge of self

Appreciation of others

Ability to adjust to change

Respect for law and authority

Clarification of values

Appreciation of the achievements of man.[4]

In our current era of accountability, in school districts throughout the nation citizens and educators are working together to develop the basic goals of their schools. For example, this set developed in 1973 by the Jefferson County, Colo., school district is undoubtedly typical:

Each student will:

Master the basic skills for continued learning

Develop a sense of responsibility. Act with understanding and respect toward others as individuals

Develop his unique talents and his sense of worth, well-being, and happiness to the fullest

Become actively prepared to cope with change

Develop the skills and attitudes necessary to earn a living and function as a contributing member of society.

The annual Gallup Polls on education also provide current data on the public's perceptions of the job of schools. Here is a question from the 1972 poll of a national sample of adults:[5]

People have different reasons why they want their children to get an education. What are the chief reasons that come to your mind?

Here are the responses and the percentages of respondents mentioning each in some form:

1. To get better jobs .... 44 percent

2. To get along better with people at all levels
of society .... 43 percent

3. To make more money—achieve
financial success .... 38 percent

4. To attain self-satisfaction .... 21 percent

5. To stimulate their minds .... 15 percent

6. Miscellaneous reasons .... 11 percent

This information has been reported to illustrate that the climate goals at the outset of this section are supportive of the aims of American education. They represent routes for achieving the larger purposes of schooling. One climate goal pertains to productivity as it concerns academic, social, and physical development of skills, knowledge, and attitudes. Because of the importance of productivity in the developmental life of youngsters, and the fact that youth spend a large portion of their life in school, the second climate goal is equally important. This goal pertains to satisfaction—the need for a fulfilling and quality school life.

General Climate Factors

If you were to walk into a school building and try to gain a sense of its prevailing climate, what would you look for? Along what lines would you assess its positiveness or negativeness?

We suggest you look for at least eight factors, which comprise the school's climate and determine its quality. They result from an interaction of the school's programs, processes, and physical conditions.

Ideally, there should be evidence of:

1. *Respect.* Students should see themselves as persons of worth, believing that they have ideas, and that those ideas are listened to and make a difference. Teachers and administrators should feel the same way. School should be a place where there are self-respecting individuals. Respect is also due to others. In a positive climate there are no put-downs.

2. *Trust.* Trust is reflected in one's confidence that others can be counted on to behave in a way that is honest. They will do what they say they will do. There is also an element of believing others will not let you down.

3. *High Morale.* People with high morale feel good about what is happening.

4. *Opportunities for Input.* Not all persons can be involved in making the important decisions. Not always can each person be as influential as he might like to be on the many aspects of the school's programs and processes that affect him. But every person cherishes the opportunity to contribute his or her ideas, and know they have been considered. A feeling of a lack of voice is counterproductive to self-esteem and deprives the school of that person's resources.

5. *Continuous Academic and Social Growth.* Each student needs to develop additional academic, social, and physical skills, knowledge, and attitudes. (Many educators have described the growth process as achieving "developmental tasks." Educators, too, desire to improve their skills, knowledge, and attitudes in regard to their particular assignments within the school district and as cooperative members of a team.)

6. *Cohesiveness.* This quality is measured by the person's feeling toward the school. Members should feel a part of the school. They want to stay with it and have a chance to exert their influence on it in collaboration with others.

7. *School Renewal.* The school as an institution should develop improvement projects. It should be self-renewing in that it is growing, developing, and changing rather than following routines, repeating previously accepted procedures, and striving for conformity. If there is renewal, difference is seen as interesting, to be cherished. Diversity and pluralism are valued. New conditions are faced with poise. Adjustments are worked out as needed. The "new" is not seen as threatening, but as something to be examined, weighed, and its value or relevance determined. The school should be able to organize improvement projects rapidly and efficiently, with an absence of stress and conflict.

8. *Caring.* Every individual in the school should feel that some other person or persons are concerned about him as a human being. Each knows it will make a difference to

someone else if he is happy or sad, healthy or ill. (Teachers should feel that the principal cares about them even when they make mistakes or disagree. And the principal should know that the teachers—at least most of them—understand the pressures under which he or she is working and will help if they can.)

*9.

*10.

Figure 1-2 lists the factors that comprise the school's climate and determine its quality. At the center are the goals for the school's climate as presented in Figure 1-1.

Basic Human Needs within the School

If it is to be successful—productive and satisfying—any institution must provide opportunities for students, faculty, staff, and administrators to fulfill their basic human needs. An effective, wholesome climate cannot exist without meeting such needs. In a sense, the basic needs are an additional means of viewing many of the climate factors just described.

No school organization can possess a wholesome climate without providing for the essential needs of its students and educators:

Physiological needs for involvement in learning. These involve the school's physical plant including heat, light, safety from hazards such as fire, and relatively uncrowded conditions.

Safety needs pertain to security from physical and psychological abuse or assault from others in or around the school.

Acceptance and friendship needs from other students, teachers, staff, and administrators.

Achievement and recognition needs in regard to one's endeavors.

Needs to maximize one's potential or to achieve at the highest possible level.

---

*The authors do not believe the factors listed above, or the other listings used to describe the school's climate, are all-inclusive. Readers may wish to delete or add items, and space is provided for them to do so.

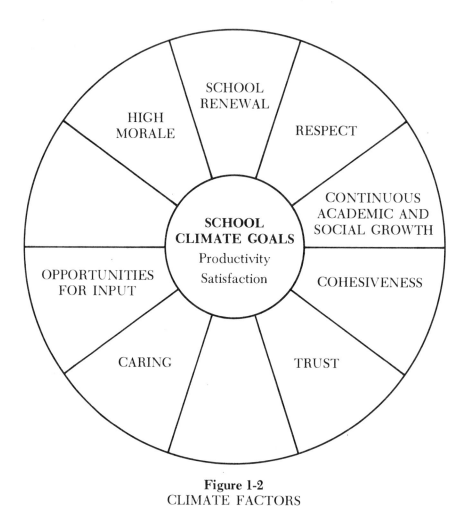

Figure 1-2
CLIMATE FACTORS

These needs, which are charted in Figure 1-3, concern the desire of each person for acceptance, identity, and security.

Through their interaction, the programs, processes, and physical conditions of the school must provide for each of the basic needs if a wholesome climate is to develop. Should a school deal only with safety needs, for example, it is not likely that trust, respect, high morale, and the like would develop. Safety might be provided by seeing to it that students sit quietly at their desks all day long. But such an approach to safety would do nothing to build trust, encourage innovativeness, or contribute to high morale. Further, a school that has outstanding opportunities for learning, a beautiful physical plant, and involvement processes for making decisions, but has students being physically attacked in the restrooms or teachers fearing for their safety is not likely to develop a wholesome climate.

BASIC HUMAN NEEDS OF STUDENTS AND EDUCATORS				
Physiological Needs	Safety Needs	Acceptance and Friendship Needs	Achievement and Recognition Needs	Needs to Maximize One's Potential

Figure 1-3

Focus of School Climate Improvement Projects

It is not likely that a school can directly embark upon precise projects to improve trust, respect, cohesiveness, caring, opportunities for input, high morale, school renewal, and continuous growth. These are not factors that the school is likely to have been working on directly, even if it could. They are universal, and their quality is actually a result of the practices and programs of the more specific school operations within the areas of program, process, and material determinants described in the following section.

School Climate Determinants

Described below are eighteen features of a school's operations that largely determine the quality of the factors and goals (see Figures 1-1 and 1-2) that comprise climate. It is by improving these eighteen school climate determinants that school improvement projects can most easily be developed and evaluated.

SCHOOL CLIMATE DETERMINANTS		
Program Determinants	Process Determinants	Material Determinants
Opportunities for Active Learning	Problem Solving Ability	Adequate Resources
Individualized Performance Expectations	Improvement of School Goals	Supportive and Efficient Logistical System
Varied Learning Environments	Identifying and Working with Conflicts	Suitability of School Plant
Flexible Curriculum and Extracurricular Activities	Effective Communications	
Support and Structure Appropriate to Learner's Maturity	Involvement in Decision Making	
Rules Cooperatively Determined	Autonomy with Accountability	
Varied Reward Systems	Effective Teaching-Learning Strategies	
	Ability to Plan For the Future	

Figure 1-4

The determinants are divided into three major categories: program, process, and material determinants. Figure 1-4, which appears on page 12, indicates the determinants.

Note that the listings of Figure 1-4 and the descriptions of the determinants provide space for addition of items that might be pertinent to a particular school.

In Chapter VI, each determinant is described at greater length, and examples are given to show what might be expected for each program, process, or material determinant. (These illustrations have been contributed by many practicing school principals and staff members involved in CFK Ltd.-sponsored Principal as the School's Climate Leader projects.)

Program Determinants of a positive school climate include:

1. *Opportunities for active learning* in which students are totally involved in the process, both physically and mentally, and are able to demonstrate an ability to use their knowledge and skills.

2. *Individualized performance expectations* that are reasonable, flexible, and take into account individual differences. Individuals are frequently encouraged to set their own performance goals. Care is taken to allow for differences while at the same time providing maximum challenges for fully motivating the individual.

3. *Varied learning environments*, which avoid a single, standard mode of instruction, class size, or atmosphere. Schools within schools and alternative programming are considered potential processes for developing optional environments.

4. *Flexible curriculum and extracurricular activities* that provide a wide variety of pace and content options for learners. It is not assumed that all learners in a group have the same content needs or that most will learn at the same rate. Extracurricular activities should serve all students and be subject to constant redevelopment as students' needs change. To the greatest extent possible, such activities should be offered on an open-enrollment basis.

5. *Support and structure appropriate to learner's maturity* in which the school designs its programs, activities, and requirements so they are consistent with the everchanging intellectual, social, and physical developmental character-

istics of youth as they grow. Educators practice the principles of child and adolescent growth and development.

6. *Rules cooperatively determined* involving educators and students in the development of rules and regulations that are clearly stated and viewed as reasonable and desirable by those affected.

7. *Varied reward systems,* which minimize punishment and emphasize positive reinforcement of effective behavior. The school should recognize the need for and provide a variety of ways in which students and educators can be productive and successful.

8.

9.

Process determinants of a positive school climate include:

1. *Problem solving ability* in which skills are adequately developed to reach effective solutions quickly. Problems should stay solved, and the solving mechanism should be maintained and strengthened. There should be well-developed structures and procedures for sensing the existence of problems, for inventing solutions, for implementing them, and for evaluating their effectiveness.

2. *Improvement of school goals* in which they are clearly stated and understood by students, parents, and educators. Goals should serve as reference points for making decisions, organizing school improvement projects, and guiding day-to-day operations. The school should record all goals and continuously update them. Students, staff members, and administrators are encouraged to develop personal goals directed toward their own growth within the context of the school program.

3. *Identifying and working with conflicts* in a way that recognizes that conflict is natural and that it occurs within individuals, between them, and between groups. Conflict is not a problem unless it mounts up, is not faced, and is allowed to fester. In a favorable climate, conflict is accurately identified and effectively worked on.

4. *Effective communications,* which enhance interpersonal

relationships among and between educators and students and parents rather than causing alienation, isolation, misunderstanding, fear, and frustration. Communication involves sending, receiving, and understanding feelings and ideas openly and honestly. It is a multidimensional process, unrestricted by hierarchies or other imposed or imaginary barriers. There should be emphasis on sharing and problem solving, as well as a concern for purposeful listening.

5. *Involvement in decision making* in which opportunity to improve the school exists for students, educators, interested parents, and others. Persons affected by a decision need an opportunity to provide input. Decisions should be based on pertinent information, and decision processes should be clearly specified and understood by all. A variety of decision-making models should be used and the entire process reviewed periodically for effectiveness and efficiency.

6. *Autonomy with accountability,* which balances the freedom of being independent and self-governing with the necessity and desirability of being responsible for actions through reporting and explaining processes in achieving goals and objectives. This equity is vital not only to the school as an organization, but to educators and students as individuals and as working groups.

7. *Effective teaching-learning strategies* in which goals for teaching-learning situations are clearly stated and educators seek evaluative feedback from students and other educators. Teachers should recognize that students have varied learning styles and should attempt to employ methods that consider these styles as well as student maturity. Students should have frequent opportunity to choose from a variety of learning activities. Inquiry should be encouraged, and a system should exist to evaluate teaching strategies.

8. *Ability to plan for the future* is a characteristic whereby the school determines and plans for its immediate and long-range future. In this process, the school's educators and clientele analyze the general course of the education program at their school, and deliberately plan desirable changes and modifications in the school's programs, services, and processes. It involves planning skills and a future orientation—

the attempt to project conditions as the educators and clientele want them to be.

9.

10.

Material determinants of a positive school climate include:

1. *Adequate resources,* which include able educators and support for them and students through provision of instructional material centers and laboratories, desirable classroom or learning-area equipment, furniture, textbooks and references, other materials, and adequate expendable supplies.

2. *Supportive and efficient logistical system,* which is designed to help people be productive in achieving the school, curriculum, and extracurricular activity goals. A responsive system enhances morale. Procedures should enable individuals to efficiently acquire needed material resources. Educators should be able to get commonly used resources rapidly. The system should provide quality in such areas as student scheduling, and in custodial, maintenance, secretarial, purchasing, budgeting, and accounting services. Each individual should know what he can and cannot expect of a school's logistical system.

3. *Suitability of school plant* in which the institution modifies the physical plant as program and human needs change, keeping building decor attractive by use of color, furniture arrangement, and displays of student work.

4.

5.

Chapter VI, "School Climate Determinants," further discusses each of the above eighteen characteristics. Chapter VII shows how a school might initiate a process of developing its own set of definitions and climate determinants, particularly relevant to its own needs and perceptions.

Summary

The preceding material, along with Figures 1-1, 1-2, 1-3, and 1-4, provide a conceptual overview and definition of the school's climate. In summary form, Figure 1-5 combines the concepts.

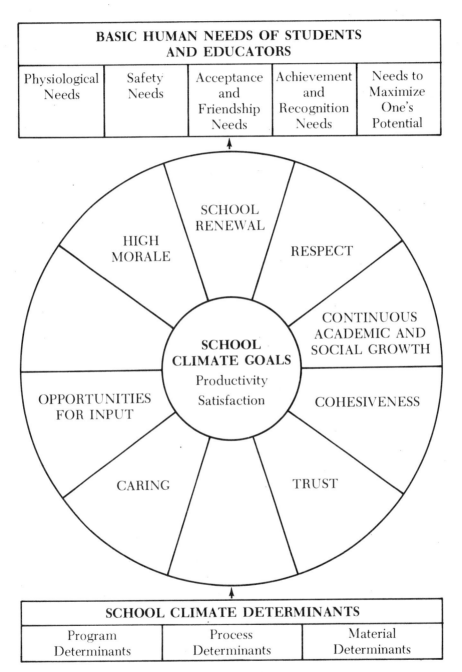

Figure 1-5
THE CLIMATE OF THE SCHOOL

The CFK Ltd. School Climate Profile

The CFK Ltd. School Climate Profile of Chapter V, pages 51-72, is designed to assist school administrators, teachers, and others in assessing the overall climate of their schools. It is so organized that the quality of each of the determinants of a school's climate and the factors of the school's climate previously described can be assessed. It is important to note that the profile instrument does not pretend to include an item on every factor that might be significant. The value of the instrument is more as an overall school climate assessment tool rather than as a definitive or exhaustive survey. It can provide data to help in deciding what elements of the climate should be looked at more intensively. Further, the instrument is designed to obtain data concerning people's perceptions of each climate element and factor and how they believe each might be.

Rate Your School's Climate

A brief rating scale appears on pages 19-22, which the reader can use at this point to record his perceptions of the climate of his school.

Next Steps

It is hoped that completion of the following rating scale will help the reader to determine ways in which the remaining parts of this book—dealing largely with climate improvement activities—can be useful. It is suggested that he again refer to "How to Use this Book" on pages x-xi.

Chapter II, which follows, issues a challenge to the administrator to identify himself as a climate leader and to view school climate improvement as one of his key functions in improving his school's learning environment.

RATE YOUR SCHOOL'S CLIMATE

School Climate Factors	To What Degree is this Factor a Strength or Weakness of Your School? It is — VW—Very Weak W—Weak U—Unknown S—Strong VS—Very Strong (Circle the Appropriate Letters)					Reference: For a Description of this Factor, See Page—
General Climate Factors						
Respect	VW	W	U	S	VS	7
Trust	VW	W	U	S	VS	7
High Morale	VW	W	U	S	VS	8
Opportunities for Input	VW	W	U	S	VS	8
Continuous Academic and Social Growth	VW	W	U	S	VS	8
Cohesiveness	VW	W	U	S	VS	8
School Renewal	VW	W	U	S	VS	8
Caring	VW	W	U	S	VS	8
	VW	W	U	S	VS	
	VW	W	U	S	VS	

RATE YOUR SCHOOL'S CLIMATE (Cont'd)

School Climate Determinants	To What Degree is this Determinant a Strength or Weakness of Your School? It is— VW—Very Weak W—Weak U—Unknown S—Strong VS—Very Strong (Circle the Appropriate Letters)					Reference: For a Description of this Determinant, See Page—
Program Determinants						
Opportunities for Active Learning	VW	W	U	S	VS	13
Individualized Performance Expectations	VW	W	U	S	VS	13
Varied Learning Environments	VW	W	U	S	VS	13
Flexible Curriculum and Extracurricular Activities	VW	W	U	S	VS	13
Support and Structure Appropriate to Learner's Maturity	VW	W	U	S	VS	13-14
Rules Cooperatively Determined	VW	W	U	S	VS	14
Varied Reward Systems	VW	W	U	S	VS	14
	VW	W	U	S	VS	
	VW	W	U	S	VS	

RATE YOUR SCHOOL'S CLIMATE (Cont'd)

School Climate Determinants	To What Degree is this Determinant a Strength or Weakness of Your School? It is— VW—Very Weak W—Weak U—Unknown S—Strong VS—Very Strong (Circle the Appropriate Letters)					Reference: For a Description of this Determinant, See Page—
Process Determinants						
Problem Solving Ability	VW	W	U	S	VS	14
Continuous Improvement of School Goals	VW	W	U	S	VS	14
Identifying and Working with Conflicts	VW	W	U	S	VS	14
Effective Communications	VW	W	U	S	VS	14-15
Involvement in Decision Making	VW	W	U	S	VS	15
Autonomy with Accountability	VW	W	U	S	VS	15
Effective Teaching-Learning Strategies	VW	W	U	S	VS	15
Ability to Plan for the Future	VW	W	U	S	VS	15-16
	VW	W	U	S	VS	
	VW	W	U	S	VS	

RATE YOUR SCHOOL'S CLIMATE (Cont'd)

School Climate Determinants	To What Degree is this Determinant a Strength or Weakness of Your School? It is — VW—Very Weak W—Weak U—Unknown S—Strong VS—Very Strong (Circle the Appropriate Letters)					Reference: For a Description of this Determinant, See Page—
Material Determinants						
Adequate Resources	VW	W	U	S	VS	16
Supportive and Efficient Logistical System	VW	W	U	S	VS	16
Suitability of School Plant	VW	W	U	S	VS	16
	VW	W	U	S	VS	
	VW	W	U	S	VS	

CHAPTER II

Improving the School's Climate: A Challenge to the School Administrator

The School Administrator as a Climate Leader

Considerable evidence exists that a school is the shadow of its administrator. If schools accept the premise that they should provide a designed and humane environment for students and staff, administrators likely will need to develop additional leadership skills, knowledge, and attitudes.

Typically, the principal, over the years, has been viewed as the school's instructional leader. Improvement of instruction has been seen as his paramount job.

The principalship at both elementary and secondary school levels has been invariably viewed by authors of research reports and administration textbooks as primarily a leadership position, with particular reference to the improvement and supervision of instruction.[1]

For the most part, efforts to improve designs for the principalship have suggested means to improve the principal's contributions as an instructional leader.

The authors challenge the preceding quotation and argue that the school administrator is first and foremost a climate leader and that his key function is improvement of the school's climate or learning environment.

School improvement begins with the administrator. This may be in opposition to the concept of many school leaders who are concerned about change—but change for others such as students, faculty, and staff rather than for themselves. If the administrator is to improve himself, his first task becomes one of identifying his strengths and weaknesses as a climate leader. Such a role is exemplified by the administrator who personifies the school's philosophy, demonstrating by his actions that it is possible to practice what is preached.

H. Thomas James puts the foregoing into perspective with this statement:

> Real authority for leadership must be earned in a society that prefers persuasion to force, and leadership is a privilege conferred out of trust for relevant knowledge, competent behavior, and demonstrated ability. . . .[2]

The job of the administrator as a climate leader is to provide leadership and an accountability system consistent with the school's philosophy for school-based task forces of staff, administrator, parents, and students. In working with colleagues and the school's clientele, he provides the basic leadership for:

Assessing school climate improvement needs

Setting goals to describe needed improvements

Reducing goals to manageable projects with measurable objectives

Devising strategies for attaining the objectives

Implementing these strategies

Evaluating progress by establishing check-points and periodically monitoring achievements

Improving each project in light of evaluative processes.

These processes are discussed in Chapter III, "Becoming a School Climate Leader."

> Research is a high-hat word that scares a lot of people. It needn't. It is rather simple. Essentially research is nothing but a state of mind—a friendly, welcoming attitude toward change . . . going out to look for change instead of waiting for it to come. Research, for practical men, is an effort to do things

better and not to be caught asleep at the switch. . . . It is the problem-solving mind as contrasted with the let-well-enough-alone mind. . . . It is the "tomorrow" mind instead of the "yesterday" mind.

—Charles F. Kettering

School Climate Improvement Rationale

It is often desirable for the school administrator to develop a rationale as to the significance of improving school climate. Chapter VIII, "Why Do It: Rationale for Organizing School Climate Improvements," consists of a resource of concepts and quotations. Many of these may be useful to the administrator in clarifying his own thinking and in developing presentations he may need to make regarding school climate improvement.

Programs for Educating School Administrators as Climate Leaders

Admittedly, the history of providing designed opportunities for school administrators to gain the necessary abilities for providing climate improvement leadership is brief.

The ideas and concepts presented here are not figments of the authors' imaginations. This book is, in fact, based upon the practices of approximately twenty-five school systems throughout the nation, which have actually been operating elementary and secondary school climate improvement programs since 1968 in association with CFK Ltd. In organizing such programs, each school system essentially accomplishes the following:

A district administrator is designated to provide leadership. This educator involves other administrators in organizing a plan of action.

Given a sketch of the district's program, interested school administrators volunteer to join the endeavor.

Collegial teams are organized consisting of from eight to twelve administrators, and each team organizes learning activities.

Each participating administrator develops his own professional growth program directly related to school climate improvement projects.

Participating administrators refine their school district's program yearly.

The authors are either associated with one of the participating districts or have been working with a number of these school systems. Further, representatives of more than forty-five school systems involved in CFK Ltd. programs have not only reviewed, but contributed to this publication.

The CFK Ltd. Occasional Paper, *Individualizing Administrator Continuing Education*, by Edward Brainard, is designed to show administrators how to organize such programs in their school districts.

Chapter III, "Becoming a School Climate Leader," provides a range of options for directly dealing with school climate problems and inaugurating improvement projects. In another sense, Chapter III can be considered as a self-instruction program. It is especially potent when it is used along with Chapter IV through VIII of this book. In short, they deal with these questions:

How does one know if a school's climate is positive?

How can the school's climate be improved?

What are the administrator's responsibilities for improving the climate?

What processes might he use to provide the leadership for inaugurating school climate improvement projects?

Has Your School's Climate Been Improved?
A Checklist for the School Administrator

During the past two years, what climate improvements have occurred at your school?

This rating scale lists characteristics that determine the nature, quality, and wholesomeness of the school's climate. It is designed to assist the reader in analyzing the extent to which improvements have been recently organized in a planned, comprehensive, and highly conscious manner for the purpose of systematically improving the school's climate. While many schools make improvements, they are often the result of happenstance or crisis.

School Climate Determinants	During the Past Two Years *Planned* Climate Improvement Programs have Occurred—				
	Regularly	Occasionally	Rarely	Not at All	Unknown
Program Determinants					
Opportunities for Active Learning					
Individualized Performance Expectations					
Varied Learning Environments					
Flexible Curriculum and Extra-curricular Activities					
Support and Structure Appropriate to Learner's Maturity					
Rules Cooperatively Determined					
Varied Reward Systems					
Process Determinants					
Problem-solving Ability					
Continuous Improvement of School Goals					
Identifying and Working with Conflicts					
Effective Communications					
Involvement in Decision Making					
Autonomy with Accountability					
Effective Teaching-Learning Strategies					
Ability to Plan for the Future					
Material Determinants					
Adequate Resources					
Supportive and Efficient Logistical System					
Suitability of School Plant					

CHAPTER III

Becoming a School Climate Leader

Leadership Services

The school administrator makes the difference. For example:
Faculties that move rapidly from theory to practice are led by self-directed, change-oriented administrators. Very simply stated, the principal knows where he is going. He reads widely, listens to teachers and other experts, and reflects on the pressures that come from many sources. He has developed a philosophy of education.[1]

Regarding the school's climate and its improvement, in involving faculty, staff, parents, and students the administrator should provide seven basic leadership services. As listed in Chapter II, these are:

Assessing school climate improvement needs

Setting goals to describe needed improvements

Reducing goals to manageable projects with measurable objectives

Devising strategies for attaining the objectives

Implementing these strategies

Evaluating progress by establishing check-points and periodically monitor achievements

Improving each project in light of evaluative processes

The ideas included in this chapter, together with those of the remaining chapters of this book, provide guidelines and specific school climate improvement activities. Referring to the above list these suggestions are especially helpful for:

Assessing climate improvement needs

Setting goals

Devising strategies

Implementing strategies

Evaluating progress.[2]

Selection of an Initial Emphasis

How does one begin? An individual may start by assessing his own personal/professional leadership behavior and using these data to inaugurate a plan for improving his personal/professional skills and knowledge as a climate leader. Or he may begin by assessing the overall organizational climate of his school and using these data to isolate a few major climate problems that are the thrust of his and the staff's improvement efforts. Or he may wish to undertake both simultaneously.

The administrator may wish to use the following checklist to clarify his own orientation for initial efforts.

A Checklist: Initial Emphasis

I believe I should start our school climate improvement project by using:

___ *Emphasis Option 1:* An administrator looking at himself. The administrator assesses his personal/professional leadership skills using data from assessment processes to generate a personal/professional improvement plan to upgrade his skills as a climate leader.

___ *Emphasis Option 2:* An administrator looking at his school by assessing the overall climate of the school. He uses these data to isolate a few major climate problems in the school.

He forms planning teams to generate projects/activities to overcome climate problems that have been identified.

_____ *Emphasis Option 3:* An administrator looking at himself and his school. The principal chooses to undertake both of the above options simultaneously.

With the selection of an initial emphasis, six sequential goals or steps follow. They are applicable to each emphasis.

Six Suggested Sequential Goals for Becoming A School Climate Leader and Initiating Climate Improvement Projects

Goal 1: Expand your understanding of school climate, participative management, and the leader's role in creating an improved climate.

Options for Attaining This Goal	How to Go About It
Read books, articles, monographs on organizational climate and participative management.	Refer to Activity 1 in Chapter IV of this book for selected readings on school climate and participative management. (See page 38.)
Talk to practicing principals, superintendents, and professors actively involved in school climate improvement projects.	Refer to Activity 2 in Chapter IV, and Chapter IX, "Human Resources," for names of practicing administrators and professors involved in school climate improvement (See pages 38 and 133-138.)
Visit elementary and secondary schools that have undertaken school climate improvement projects.	Refer to Activity 3 in Chapter IV, and Chapter IX, "Human Resources," for names of schools involved in climate improvement projects. (See pages 38 and 133-138.)

Goal 1 (Cont'd.)

Options for Attaining This Goal

How to Go About It

Solicit human resources to visit your school and work with your staff, school board, parent groups, and others on school climate improvement projects.

Goal 2: Decide whether you really want to commit yourself to be a climate leader in your school, your school district, and your community.

Options for Attaining This Goal

How to Go About It

Complete a brief analysis of the attitudes and skills you will need in order to become a climate leader in your school. Are you then willing to commit yourself to learn and practice these attitudes and skills?

Refer to Activity 21 in Chapter IV, and Chapter IX, "Instruments," for "Values Clarification" exercise. (See pages 48 and 139.)

Read McGregor's Theory X and Y. Assess what you'd have to do to have a Theory Y school. Can you gear yourself up?

Refer to Activity 4 in Chapter IV, and Chapter IX, "Articles, Books, and Reports," for McGregor's article. (See pages 38 and 130.)

List the projects that might be undertaken to make your school more of a Theory Y school. How do you see yourself working with people to get these projects done?

Refer to Activity 14, Chapter IV, and Chapter IX, "Articles, Books, and Reports." (See pages 46 and 130.)

Do a force field analysis on your becoming a climate leader in your school, district, and community.

Refer to Activity 11, Chapter IV, for directions on conducting a force field analysis (See pages 44-45.)

Goal 3: Clarify and commit yourself to the leadership role that *you* want to assume in *your* school, in *your* district, in *your* community.

Options for Attaining This Goal

How to Go About It

Write a brief statement describing your perception of the leadership role you want to assume. Try it out on small groups of colleagues, including your supervisors.

Ask your staff or a smaller support team from within your staff to use the LBDQ to assess your leadership role.

See Chapter IX, "Instruments," for information on obtaining the LBDQ. (See page 138.)

Design a written personal/professional growth plan to implement your desired leadership role. Form a collegial team to assist you with your personal/professional growth.

Refer to Activities 6 and 14, Chapter IV, and Chapter IX, "Articles, Books, and Reports," for personal/professional growth plan format and paper on forming collegial teams. (See pages 39 and 46-47 and 130.)

Goal 4: Identify and prioritize climate problems in your school.

Options for Attaining This Goal

How to Go About It

Read paper on *Self and School Assessment Processes.*

Refer to Activity 5, Chapter IV, and Chapter IX, "CFK Ltd. Occasional Papers," on how to get started. (See pages 39 and 129.)

Goal 4: (Cont'd.)

Options for Attaining This Goal	How to Go About It
Conduct informal discussions with staff members and students to identify climate problem areas—what our school is and can be.	Refer to Activity 10, Chapter IV for use of "Images of Potentiality." (See pages 40-44.)
Utilize a consensus task approach to identify and prioritize climate problems in your school.	Refer to Activity 7, Chapter IV, and Chapter IX, "Articles, Books, and Reports," for explanation of 1-3-6 consensus task approach. (See pages 39 and 130.)
Involve staff and students in brainstorming sessions to identify climate problems and have them suggest alternatives.	Refer to Activity 12, Chapter IV, for explanation of brainstorming. (See pages 45-46.)
Administer standardized organizational climate instrument in your school.	Refer to Activity 25, Chapter IV, and Chapter IX, "Instruments," for information on OCDQ. (See pages 49 and 138.)
Administer school climate profile in your school and prioritize problem areas.	Refer to Activity 16, Chapter IV, and Chapter V for copy of The CFK Ltd. School Climate Profile Instrument. (See pages 47 and 51-72.)

Goal 5: Involve people in improving your school's climate.

Options for Attaining This Goal	How to Go About It
Commit yourself and work with staff members on a program of personal/professional growth.	Refer to Activity 22, Chapter IV, and Chapter IX, "CFK Ltd. Occasional Papers." (See pages 48 and 129.)

Goal 5: (Cont'd.)

Options for Attaining This Goal	How to Go About It
Utilize a planning model to initiate climate improvement projects.	Refer to Activities 22, 23, and 24, Chapter IV, and Chapter IX, for rationale and use of three simple planning models. (See pages 48-49 and 129-130.)
Organize collegial teams to undertake individual- and/or group-initiated school climate improvement projects.	Refer to Activity 6, Chapter IV, and Chapter IX, "CFK Ltd. Occasional Papers," for how to initiate collegial teams for school climate improvement projects. (See pages 39 and 129.)

Goal 6: Design and implement maintenance and feedback systems for individuals and teams involved in school climate improvement.

Options for Attaining This Goal	How to Go About It
Establish individual accountability reports for each staff member undertaking a program of personal/professional growth.	Place the dates of these sessions on the master activities calendar and hold to them.
Design simplified techniques for teams to report back to staff, board, and community.	Refer to Activity 17, Chapter IV, for discussion of "Reality Check with Kitchen Cabinet." (See page 47.)
Have specified outsiders/insiders conduct regular checkups on the quality of your organization's climate and report back to staff, and, where appropriate, to the board of education and community.	Refer to Chapter IX, "Human Resources," for people available to you to assess the quality of your school's climate. (See pages 133-138.)

Goal 6: (Cont'd.)

Options for Attaining This Goal	**How to Go About It**
Have staff follow a problem-solving format to present feedback data.	Refer to Chapter IX, "Articles, Books, and Reports," for reference to *Toward the Human Element,* 2nd ed., for explanation of problem solving process. (See page 130.)

To summarize, a principal begins to improve the quality of his school's climate by:

1. Starting small—undertaking low-risk projects first
2. Making an assessment of a) personal leadership skills and b) organizational climate
3. Developing a plan of action via a personal growth plan and/or isolating a few major organizational problem areas and forming a planning team
4. Using a planning model
5. Getting staff, students, and community involved when possible
6. Developing projects that can be accomplished, thus guaranteeing success.

CHAPTER IV

Activities for Becoming
a Climate Leader
and Developing
School Climate
Improvement Projects

Introduction

The selection of emphasis and subsequent refinement of intent suggested in the six goals and their activities described in Chapter III can be viewed as analysis—a crystalization of where the administrator is, who he is, and how well he is equipped to undertake the functions and responsibilities of school climate leadership. In Chapter IV, the focus shifts to synthesis, with a series of twenty-five activities ranging from enterprises as passive as reading (Activity 1) to ones as complex as organizing and conducting an "Images of Potentiality" session (Activity 10). Use of all (or combinations of) these activities can bring various associates into the arena of the administrator's efforts and ideas, and steer school climate improvement onto a track wider than one man could hope to make it.

Activity 1: Readings

One might consider a number of readings that are listed below. Complete bibliographical information on each may be found in Chapter IX, "Bibliography of Resources."

CFK Ltd. Occasional Paper, *The Principal as the School's Climate Leader: A New Role for the Principalship*

Crisis in the Classroom: The Remaking of American Education, by Charles E. Silberman.

Life in the Classrooms, by Philip W. Jackson.

"Humanizing the Schools: Its Meaning, The Principal's Role, and Several Approaches," *NASSP Bulletin* No. 361.

Refer to Chapter IX for additional resources.

Activity 2: Discussions with Other Principals Who are Involved in School Climate Improvement Projects

Talk with practicing administrators engaged in "climate projects." Feel free to call them on the telephone or to exchange a cassette tape with them. See Chapter IX, "Human Resources," for a listing of numerous educators who are knowledgeable about climate improvement.

Activity 3: Visit Schools Involved in School Climate Projects

Perhaps visiting a school site would be helpful for gaining ideas. Again, refer to Chapter IX, "Human Resources." Should one decide to use this option, please contact the individual representatives in advance of the visit.

Activity 4: McGregor's Theory X and Theory Y

It is generally accepted that administrators have different styles. These vary from very open and democratic on the one hand, to the very closed or authoritarian on the other. One of the better articles on this topic is, "The Human Side of Enterprise," by Douglas McGregor. In his article, there is considerable explanation about different administrative approaches, and what their various effects might be on a given organization. Refer to Chapter IX, "Articles, Books, and Reports."

Activity 5:   Self and School Assessment Process

As principals wrestle with the problem of how to get started with a school climate improvement project, one source that the authors feel is extremely valuable is a CFK Ltd. Occasional Paper, *Self and School Assessment Processes: A Guidebook for Administrators,* by Gerald Prince. This paper describes the processes a school administrator can use to isolate a school's climate improvement needs. It includes a wide variety of activities and also indicates the different kinds of circumstances in which these are usually most applicable.

Activity 6:   Establishment of an Internal Support Team and/or an External Collegial Team

As a principal undertakes to improve his school's climate, it is often very helpful to have a group of faculty members whom he trusts and feels comfortable with gathered around him to assist him in these school climate improvement projects. The exact way these teams are formed and who is involved with them and how many, etc., will vary from situation to situation. The same is true of an "outside" support team or collegial team composed of other principals or administrators who are likewise working on school climate in their given situations. A good source addressed to the formation of an effective team is the CFK Ltd. Occasional Paper, *Administrator Renewal: The Leadership Role and Collegial Team Development,* by Vivian Geddes. Refer to Chapter IX for reference.

Activity 7:   One, Three, Six, Processes of Consensus Task

An individual lists the ten most significant problems he/she believes his/her school faces today. These problems can be combined with those listed by two other people to build a composite list. Just combine the problems repeated on other lists and add the problems not held in common. Two groups of three join together into a group of six. Make a composite list. Then build a total group composite list and put it into priority order. Identify at least the top three to five problems of your school. This process is clearly outlined in *Toward the Human Element,* 2nd ed., by Carnie and Prince. Refer to Chapter IX, "Articles, Books, and Reports."

Activity 8: The Personal Value Inventory

The Personal Value Inventory is an instrument designed by the W. Clement and Jessie V. Stone Foundation as part of their Achievement Motivation Program. The instrument is self-administered and is useful in unobtrusively finding one's personal values. Two different approaches for determining personal values are available. Directions for administering the instrument are contained in the document. Refer to Chapter IX, "Instruments."

Activity 9: Personal Values vs. Institutional Values

This instrument is used to check perceived personal values regarding an education for students in relationship to the perceived operation of the school. There are twenty-five items in the survey, and users mark each of the items twice to show the congruence or divergence between what they believe should be and what they believe is. This instrument is available from Nueva Day School and Learning Center. Refer to Chapter IX, "Instruments."

Activity 10: Images of Potentiality

One interesting approach to getting staff and students involved in school climate improvement is to solicit their help in creating "images of potentiality." It may serve as a more positive, creative starting point than the traditional one of identifying *problems* to be solved, or *needs* to be met.

Following is a design for such an Images of Potentiality session:

Participants: All teachers, all support staff (secretaries, custodians, cafeteria workers), all administrators, a representative group of students (roughly comparable to the number of teachers), and a representative group of parents.

Time: Two and one-half hours.

Location: Large room with small tables for clusters of six persons at each table.

Grouping: For the purpose of generating as broad a set of images as possible, it may be helpful to form the initial clusters of six by role group; e.g., six students, six parents, six administrators, etc.

Materials: Each table should have available eight to ten sheets of newsprint paper and a large felt tipped marking pen.

Schedule of Activities:
1. Orientation (fifteen minutes): Introductory remarks about importance of school climate improvement; tie-in to any previous discussions or recommendations from faculty, student groups, etc.; possibly a brief description of some of the elements of school climate, so the participants may have an expanded vision of what areas are appropriate to think about; and, clarification of the immediate task at hand in some such words as the following:

   "Most of us keep so busy day by day trying to do the things expected of us, or solving the problems that confront us, that we have little time to think ahead to what might be a better way to live and work together.

   "In the next few minutes we are going to have a chance to think about what might be going on in this school one year from now should we be able somehow to do everything the way we'd like to do it, or the way we know it could best be done.

   "Given the kinds of things we have reviewed that are important to a positive school climate, what specific activities can you envision that might be going on in our school one year from now? Think of yourself as being on a magic carpet, hovering over the school, looking in on what is happening.

   "I'd like everyone, first, to think quietly for three minutes about what you think might be going on. Then at each table (in each group of six), put down on newsprint a brief statement about each of these images of potentiality that your group thinks is important. Try to state *what* is happening and *who* is involved.

   "You will have twenty minutes to produce your newsprint sheet or sheets. If you can list several images, do so.

   "When I call time, will each group see that their newsprint sheets are put up with masking tape on the walls of the room nearest your group so others can take a look? When you have done so, feel free to walk around the room looking at the statements produced by other groups."

2. Individual thinking about possible images (three minutes).

3. Small group sharing, and writing on newsprint their image statements describing what could be happening in this school one year from now (twenty minutes).

4. Entire group informally walking around the room, examining newsprint products of other groups (fifteen minutes).

5. Briefing (five minutes): "During the remainder of this session we shall be working with some of these images, generating ideas about what we might do in this school to bring one or more of the images to reality. In a sense, we'll just be 'testing them out' to see if we'd really like to put more extensive effort into any of them.

"The process will have three steps." (These can be listed on newsprint, overhead projector, or chalkboard.)

Stating a goal

Listing goal indicators

Brainstorming program ideas.

"First, I'll ask each group to select from its posted list of images one that they think is important enough to do further work on." (One is not bound by this exact statement. In browsing around the room he may have picked up some ideas that would improve on this.)

"Next, convert this image into a goal statement. Put it on newsprint. You have a total of ten minutes."

6. Small group work on selecting one image; converting to goal statement (ten minutes).

7. Briefing (ten minutes): For the next step, two groups will join together, one serving as consultant to the other. You may want to work this out so that each group knows with which other group it will be paired. One group can be designated "Group A," the other, "Group B."

"The next step is to get help in listing some goal indicators for your goal. A goal indicator is evidence you would accept that the goal has been reached. For example, if the goal is:

"There is meaningful involvement of teachers, students, and parents in curriculum decisions."

some of the possible goal indicators might be:

Goal	Goal Indicators
There is meaningful involvement of teachers, students, and parents in curriculum decisions.	1. A curriculum council meets regularly. Faculty, students, and the community are represented.
	2. When asked, students say they do have opportunity to influence curriculum decisions.

Group A will tell Group B what its goal is. Group B will then suggest all the possible goal indicators it thinks might relate to that goal. Group A records these on newsprint.

The groups then reverse roles. Group B tells Group A what its goal is. Group A generates goal indicators while Group B lists them.

8. Group A gets suggestions from Group B (fifteen minutes). Group B gets suggestions from Group A (fifteen minutes).

9. Briefing (five minutes): Finally, each group will return to its original location, post its goal statement and list of goal indicators so they can be seen, and spend fifteen minutes brainstorming a list of program ideas or steps that might lead to achievement of the goal.

The rules of brainstorming are:

Generate as many ideas as possible in a short period of time. Don't evaluate.

Don't elaborate or discuss each idea.

Build on one another's suggestions.

Be creative—one way-out idea may stimulate a more feasible one in someone else's mind.

(For a more detailed description of brainstorming, see Activity 12.)

Record on newsprint the program ideas as they are generated. (Two recorders may be needed to keep up.)

10. Brainstorming of program ideas (fifteen minutes).

11. Finale (twenty minutes): All groups walk around the room, examining the products of the other groups.

There is general discussion of the value of the session, and ideas about next steps.

Activity 11: Force Field Analysis

The force field analysis is an excellent problem-solving technique. The technique essentially is valuable for the following four reasons:

People considering a problem can focus on both the negative and positive aspects of the problem.

The technique helps individuals focus on the issue rather than on individual personality characteristics.

The technique aids in getting at causes of problems rather than at effects of problems.

The technique aids in getting at priority concerns enabling people to put their energies where the payoff will be the greatest.

A brief description of force field analysis follows:

For purposes of simulation, let's presume that the principal has determined that many students find school a punishing experience; that is, many students find school a place where they have few successful experiences. After talking over this concern with other people, the group may decide that all students should have (as a goal) at least one successful experience each day. They may also proceed with a force field analysis to determine how it is possible to put prose into practice. The principal may lead the group in the discussion.

To get movement toward this goal, something has to change. According to Kurt Lewin, originator of the "force field" concept, any state of affairs stays just as it is because there is a whole set of forces pressing against each other (forces that might support movement toward the goal, if given a chance; and forces opposing or resisting movement toward the goal). These forces are now in balance in the field of forces (by eliminating or reducing some resisting forces, adding new supporting forces, etc.).

To use this force field concept, therefore, the first step is to identify the forces, using a chart like the following:

Forces supporting or working toward achievement of the goal.		Forces resisting or working against achievement of the goal.	Goal: provide each child with a successful experience each day.
1. 2. 3. 4. 5.	Current status with respect to the goal	1. 2. 3. 4. 5.	

When all the forces that are operating *currently* have been identified, the list of forces should be examined to determine:

Which forces are most important; i.e., have the greatest influence.

Which forces are most likely to be open to change; i.e., which are worth working on.

On the basis of these two factors, the forces can be ranked in priority as to which should be given attention first, second, etc.

Finally, the priority items should be "brainstormed" to consider alternatives for resolving the issues or changing the impact of the forces deemed most important.

See Activity 12 below for discussion of brainstorming technique.

Activity 12: Brainstorming

Brainstorming is a technique often used by individuals or groups to generate imaginative and creative solutions to problems. The technique encourages everyone to generate as many options as possible. Anything is acceptable as a potential solution. No one is to make a value judgment regarding the feasibility of any idea presented at a brainstorming session. No one in the group should make a statement such as, "that doesn't work because. . . ." This kind of comment is unacceptable, and the leader should point this out. The brainstorming technique usually makes it possible for otherwise timid members of a group to participate, because they realize they cannot be "wrong," or that they will not be "put down" by other members in the group for offering what might be considered a "dumb" idea. Before engaging in brainstorming activities, it is sometimes helpful to engage in a few warmup exercises to give people a feel for the approach. One exercise that people might try is to consider "how can two train cars full of ping-pong balls cut in half be used creatively." Exercises of this kind are both fun and helpful in "loosening up" a group.

In recording the results from a brainstorm session, it is usually best to use newsprint or chalkboard so that everyone can see the ideas that are generated, and may be stimulated to building on previous ideas. Perhaps two recorders will be needed to keep up.

Following the brainstorm, the group may wish to go back over the items and group them, prioritize them, or evaluate their potential.

Activity 13: Establishing Support Teams

A support team is generally considered to be a small group of people within an individual school. Members of this team possess a common interest and are committed to work on the team. Two types of teams are present in most successful programs—the collegial team and the development support team. Discussion regarding the collegial team is available in the CFK Ltd. Occasional Paper by Vivian Geddes. Refer to Chapter IX, "CFK Ltd. Occasional Papers."

Activity 14: Our Typical Behavior

Our Typical Behavior is an attitudinal instrument that appears on pages 70-73 of *Diagnosing Professional Climate of Schools*, by Robert S. Fox, et al. (Refer to Chapter IX, "Articles, Books, and Reports.") The tool is used to determine how closely the principal and the staff members agree on the reactions of staff to different situations that occur in the school. For example, staff members and the principal both might respond to a question such as, "What would be the typical behavior of staff members if a teacher offered an innovative suggestion for change at a staff meeting?" By comparing the principal's response with the mean responses from the staff, the principal is able to determine how well he reads the social climate. He also gets some notions about areas where work on agreement of purpose may be desirable.

Activity 15: Small Group Discussions Regarding What Is and What Should Be.

The following chart is an easy format to help a small group readily identify what is, what ought to be, and the need.

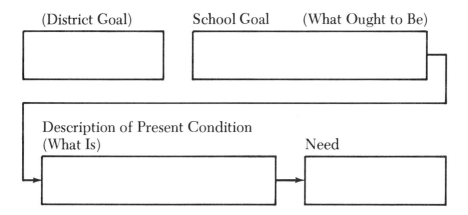

A good reference for this activity is the CFK Ltd. Occasional Paper, *Individualizing Administrator Continuing Education*, by Edward Brainard. Refer to Chapter IX.

Activity 16: Administration of School Climate Profile

Refer to Chapter V, *The CFK Ltd. School Climate Profile*, for copy of the instrument and directions for its administration.

Activity 17: Reality Check with "Kitchen Cabinet"

A "kitchen cabinet" is a small group of people, representative of the various segments of the community, who will serve as a sounding board against which you may try ideas.

The group should be one which feels comfortable to level with you, whose reactions you sincerely solicit, and whose judgments you will consider carefully.

The sessions you hold with this cabinet are private, and occasional as need for reactions seem desirable. The membership and the discussions are kept confidential.

Activity 18: Purdue Teacher Opinionaire

This is an excellent instrument for measuring such things as teacher rapport with principal, satisfaction with teaching, rapport among teachers, curriculum issues, community support of education, school facilities and services, community pressures, etc. This instrument is contained in the "Manual for the Purdue Teacher Opinionaire," by Bentley and Rempel. Refer to Chapter IX, "Instruments."

Activity 19: Interpretation and Synthesis of School Climate Data

Refer to Chapter V, pp. 53 to 72. The *CFK Ltd. School Climate Profile* and its Summary Form.

Activity 20: Budget Simulation Game

The budget simulation game is designed to have participants engage in a series of problem solving, shared decision making activities. Participants begin to get a feel of the difficulty in arriving at answers to complex issues. Greater respect for those who must engage in decision making is often a valuable result. The "game" is available from Nueva Day School and Learning Center, 6565 Skyline Boulevard, Hillsborough, Calif. 94010.

Activity 21: Values Clarification

The description of values clarification is contained in the Achievement Motivation Program designed by the W. Clement and Jessie V. Stone Foundation. It ties in directly with Activity 8, The Personal Value Inventory. Refer to Chapter IX, "Instruments," for information about where to obtain this set of materials.

Activity 22: Self Performance Achievement Record (SPAR)

The *Self Performance Achievement Record (SPAR)* is a plan-action-evaluation guide for those who do not have or use other planning systems. The package is self-contained and written in a programmed learning format, walking the user through each of the eight steps in the plan-action-evaluation sequence. This document is a CFK Ltd. Occasional Paper and was developed by actual participants in CFK Ltd. programs. Sample SPAR documents prepared by their administrators are included in the paper. Refer to Chapter IX, p. 129, "Self Performance Achievement Record."

Activity 23: Model for Change

The CFK Ltd. Occasional Paper, *A Guide to Planning School Improvements*, by Lawrence J. Aggerbeck, is an excellent resource for planning for change. See Chapter IX, p. 129.

Activity 24: Bell's Planning Model

Another good resource is *Toward the Human Element*, 2nd ed., by George Carnie and Gerald Prince. This model was developed and used in an actual school setting. Refer to Chapter IX, p. 130, "Articles, Books, and Reports."

Activity 25: Organizational Climate Description Questionnaire (OCDQ)

This instrument was designed to measure the organizational climate of elementary schools, though some data suggest it may be usable in secondary schools as well. "Climate" is defined loosely as an organization property analogous to personality. The instrument focuses on perceived social interaction between the principal and teachers, and among teachers. It is based on the assumption that a "desirable organization climate is one in which it is possible for leadership acts to emerge easily, from whatever source." Eight subscales are included: Disengagement, Hindrance, Esprit, Intimacy, Aloofness, Production Emphasis, Thrust, and Consideration.

Scores on these eight variables can be plotted as a profile.

CHAPTER V

The CFK LTD.
School Climate Profile

This instrument is designed to serve two purposes: (1) to provide a convenient means of assessing the school's climate factors and determinants so that initial decisions can be made about priority targets for improvement projects, and (2) to serve as a benchmark against which a school may measure climate change.

It includes a sample of five indicators for each of the climate factors and determinants identified in the conceptual scheme presented on pages 7-16 of this book. Since it does not pretend to include an item on every indicator that might be important, the instrument is more valuable as an overall school climate assessment tool than as a definitive or exhaustive survey. It can provide data to help in deciding what factors and determinants of the climate should be looked at more intensively.

The entire instrument takes about twenty to twenty-five minutes to complete, and has been packaged in four parts (each dealing with one of the aspects of the climate) in case it may prove more convenient to administer it in several brief sittings rather than all at once.

Data gained from this instrument will be much more powerful if gathered from people who see the school from different perspectives. Therefore, plans should be made to gather data from teachers, students, administrators, support staff members, and parents.

Data based on people's perceptions of how things are or how they feel about them are important. Most behavior is motivated by the individual's perceptions of reality. It should be clear, however, that other kinds of information, such as obtained from observation or behavioral analysis, would also be useful as part of a more extensive diagnostic effort.

The data provided by this profile can be analyzed in a number of interesting ways. Among them are:

1. Which climate factors or determinants are lowest on the scale? Which are the highest? Perhaps the lowest ones should be considered as candidates for climate improvement projects.
2. For which climate factors or determinants are the discrepancies between what is and what should be the largest? If there is a large discrepancy, perhaps the reasons for the dissonance should be examined.
3. Are there marked discrepancies between how one role group ranks a climate factor or determinant from the way it is ranked by another role group (either regarding what is or what should be)? If so, those discrepancies furnish stimulus for further discussion and examination.

The CFK Ltd. School Climate Profile

Copyright 1973

(This instrument is part of an extensive description and analysis of the school's climate and should be used in association with *School Climate Improvement: A Challenge for the School Administrator.*)

I am a:

___Student
___Teacher
___Parent
___Secretary, custodian, or other staff member
___Administrator in this school
___Superintendent or central administrator

Part A General Climate Factors	What Is: Almost Never / Occasionally / Frequently / Almost Always				What Should Be: Almost Never / Occasionally / Frequently / Almost Always			
	1	2	3	4	1	2	3	4

Respect

1. In this school even low achieving students are respected.

2. Teachers treat students as persons.

3. Parents are considered by this school as important collaborators.

4. Teachers from one subject area or grade level respect those from other subject areas.

5. Teachers in this school are proud to be teachers.

Trust:

1. Students feel that teachers are "on their side."

2. While we don't always agree, we can share our concerns with each other openly.

Part A General Climate Factors (Continued)	What Is:				What Should Be:			
	Almost Never	Occasionally	Frequently	Almost Always	Almost Never	Occasionally	Frequently	Almost Always
	1	2	3	4	1	2	3	4
3. Our principal is a good spokesman before the superintendent and the board for our interests and needs.								
4. Students can count on teachers to listen to their side of the story and to be fair.								
5. Teachers trust students to use good judgment.								

High Morale

1. This school makes students enthusiastic about learning.								
2. Teachers feel pride in this school and in its students.								
3. Attendance is good; students stay away only for urgent and good reasons.								
4. Parents, teachers, and students would rise to the defense of this school's program if it were challenged.								
5. I like working in this school.								

Opportunity for Input:

1. I feel that my ideas are listened to and used in this school.								
2. When important decisions are made about the programs in this school, I, personally, have heard about the plan beforehand and have been involved in some of the discussions.								
3. Important decisions are made in this school by a governing council with representation from students, faculty, and administration.								

	What Is:				What Should Be:			
Part A **General Climate Factors** **(Continued)**	Almost Never	Occasionally	Frequently	Almost Always	Almost Never	Occasionally	Frequently	Almost Always
	1	2	3	4	1	2	3	4

4. While I obviously can't have a vote on every decision that is made in this school that affects me, I do feel that I can have some important input into that decision.

5. When all is said and done, I feel that I *count* in this school.

Continuous Academic and Social Growth:

1. The teachers are "alive;" they are interested in life around them; they are doing interesting things outside of school.

2. Teachers in this school are "out in front," seeking better ways of teaching and learning.

3. Students feel that the school program is meaningful and relevant to their present and future needs.

4. The principal is growing and learning, too. He or she is seeking new ideas.

5. The school supports parent growth. Regular opportunities are provided for parents to be involved in learning activities and in examining new ideas.

Cohesiveness:

1. Students would rather attend this school than transfer to another.

2. There is a "we" spirit in this school.

	What Is:				What Should Be:			
Part A **General Climate Factors** **(Continued)**	Almost Never	Occasionally	Frequently	Almost Always	Almost Never	Occasionally	Frequently	Almost Always
	1	2	3	4	1	2	3	4
3. Administration and teachers collaborate toward making the school run effectively, there is little administrator-teacher tension.								
4. Differences between individuals and groups (both among faculty and students) are considered to contribute to the richness of the school; not as divisive influences.								
5. New students and faculty members are made to feel welcome and part of the group.								

School Renewal:

1. When a problem comes up, this school has procedures for working on it; problems are seen as normal challenges; not as "rocking the boat."								
2. Teachers are encouraged to innovate in their classroom rather than to conform.								
3. When a student comes along who has special problems, this school works out a plan that helps that student.								
4. Students are encouraged to be creative rather than to conform.								
5. Careful effort is made, when new programs are introduced, to adapt them to the particular needs of this community and this school.								

Caring:

1. There is someone in this school that I can always count on.

	What Is:				What Should Be:			
Part A **General Climate Factors** **(Continued)**	Almost Never	Occasionally	Frequently	Almost Always	Almost Never	Occasionally	Frequently	Almost Always
	1	2	3	4	1	2	3	4
2. The principal really cares about students.								
3. I think people in this school care about me as a person; are concerned about more than just how well I perform my role at school (as student, teacher, parent, etc.).								
4. School is a nice place to be because I feel wanted and needed there.								
5. Most people at this school are kind.								

The CFK Ltd. School Climate Profile
Copyright 1973

(This instrument is part of an extensive description and analysis of the school's climate and should be used in association with *School Climate Improvement: A Challenge for the School Administrator.*)

I am a:
__Student
__Teacher
__Parent
__Secretary, custodian, or other staff member
__Administrator in this school
__Superintendent or central administrator

	What Is:				What Should Be:			
Part B **Program Determinants**	Almost Never	Occasionally	Frequently	Almost Always	Almost Never	Occasionally	Frequently	Almost Always
	1	2	3	4	1	2	3	4

Active Learning:

1. Required textbooks and curriculum guides support rather than limit creative teaching and learning in our school.
2. Students help to decide learning objectives.
3. Opportunities are provided under school guidance to *do something* with what is learned.
4. Teachers are actively learning, too.
5. This school's program stimulates creative thought and expression.

Individualized Performance Expectations:

1. Each student's special abilities (intellectual, artistic, social, or manual) are challenged.

	What Is:				What Should Be:			
Part B **Program Determinants** **(Continued)**	Almost Never	Occasionally	Frequently	Almost Always	Almost Never	Occasionally	Frequently	Almost Always
	1	2	3	4	1	2	3	4
2. Teachers use a wide range of teaching materials and media.								
3. The same homework assignment is not given to all students in the class.								
4. All students are not held to the same standards.								
5. Teachers know students as individuals.								

Varied Learning Environments:

1. Many opportunities are provided for learning in individual and small-group settings, as well as in classroom-sized groups.
2. Students have opportunity to choose associations with teachers whose teaching styles are supportive of the student's learning style.
3. Teachers use a wide range of teaching materials and media.
4. The school program extends to settings beyond the school building for most students.
5. Teachers and administrators have planned individualized inservice education programs to support their own growth.

Flexible Curriculum and Extracurricular Activities:

1. The school's program is appropriate for ethnic and minority groups.

	What Is:				What Should Be:			
Part B **Program Determinants** **(Continued)**	Almost Never	Occasionally	Frequently	Almost Always	Almost Never	Occasionally	Frequently	Almost Always
	1	2	3	4	1	2	3	4

2. Teachers experiment with innovative programs.

3. Students are given alternative ways of meeting curriculum requirements.

4. Teachers are known to modify their lesson plans on the basis of student suggestions.

5. Extracurricular activities appeal to each of the various subgroups of students.

Support and Structure Appropriate to Learners' Maturity:

1. The school's program encourages students to develop self-discipline and initiative.

2. The needs of a few students for close supervision and high structure are met without making those students feel "put down."

3. The administration is supportive of students.

4. The administration is supportive of teachers.

5. Faculty and staff want to help every student learn.

Rules Cooperatively Determined:

1. The school operates under a set of rules which were worked out with students, teachers, parents, and administration all participating.

2. Rules are few and simple.

3. Teachers and their students together work out rules governing behavior in the classroom.

	What Is:				What Should Be:			
Part B **Program Determinants** **(Continued)**	Almost Never	Occasionally	Frequently	Almost Always	Almost Never	Occasionally	Frequently	Almost Always
	1	2	3	4	1	2	3	4
4. Discipline (punishment) when given is fair and related to violations of agreed-upon rules.								
5. Most students and staff members obey the school's rules.								
Varied Reward Systems:								
1. The grading system rewards each student for his effort in relationship to his own ability.								
2. Students know the criteria used to evaluate their progress.								
3. Teachers are rewarded for exceptionally good teaching.								
4. The principal is aware of and lets staff members and students know when they have done something particularly well.								
5. Most students get positive feedback from faculty and staff.								

The CFK Ltd. School Climate Profile
Copyright 1973

(This instrument is part of an extensive description and analysis of the school's climate and should be used in association with *School Climate Improvement: A Challenge for the School Administrator.*)

I am a:
__Student
__Teacher
__Parent
__Secretary, custodian, or other staff member
__Administrator in this school
__Superintendent or central administrator

Part C Process Determinants	What Is:				What Should Be:			
	Almost Never	Occasionally	Frequently	Almost Always	Almost Never	Occasionally	Frequently	Almost Always
	1	2	3	4	1	2	3	4

Problem Solving Ability:

1. Problems in this school are recognized and worked upon openly; not allowed to slide.

2. If I have a school-related problem, I feel there are channels open to me to get the problem worked on.

3. People in this school do a good job of examining a lot of alternative solutions first, before deciding to try one.

4. Ideas from various ethnic and minority groups are sought in problem-solving efforts.

5. People in this school solve problems; they don't just talk about them.

Improvement of School Goals:

1. This school has set some goals as a school for this year and I know about them.

	What Is:				What Should Be:			
Part C **Process Determinants** **(Continued)**	Almost Never	Occasionally	Frequently	Almost Always	Almost Never	Occasionally	Frequently	Almost Always
	1	2	3	4	1	2	3	4

2. I have set some personal goals for this year related to school, and I have shared these goals with someone else.

3. Community involvement is sought in developing the school's goals.

4. The goals of this school are *used* to provide direction for programs.

5. The goals of this school are reviewed and updated.

Identifying and Working with Conflicts:

1. In this school people with ideas or values different from the commonly accepted ones get a chance to be heard.

2. There are procedures open to me for going to a higher authority if a decision has been made that seems unfair.

3. This school believes there may be several alternative solutions to most problems.

4. In this school the principal tries to deal with conflict constructively; not just "keep the lid on."

5. When we have conflicts in this school, the result is constructive, not destructive.

Effective Communications:

1. Teachers feel free to communicate with the principal.

2. I feel the teachers are friendly and easy to talk to.

Part C Process Determinants (Continued)	What Is:				What Should Be:			
	Almost Never	Occasionally	Frequently	Almost Always	Almost Never	Occasionally	Frequently	Almost Always
	1	2	3	4	1	2	3	4
3. The principal talks with us frankly and openly.								
4. Teachers are available to students who want help.								
5. There is communication in our school between different groups—older teachers and younger ones; well-to-do students and poorer ones; black parents and white parents; etc.								

Involvement in Decision Making:

1. Teachers help in selection of new staff members.								
2. Parents help to decide about new school programs.								
3. Decisions that affect this school are made by the superintendent and the central staff only after opportunity has been provided for discussion and input from the school's principal, staff, and students.								
4. I have influence on the decisions within the school which directly affect me.								
5. The student government makes important decisions.								

Autonomy with Accountability:

1. Teachers, students, and parents help to evaluate this school's program.								
2. Teacher evaluation is used in improving teacher performance.								

	What Is:				What Should Be:			
Part C **Process Determinants** **(Continued)**	Almost Never	Occasionally	Frequently	Almost Always	Almost Never	Occasionally	Frequently	Almost Always
	1	2	3	4	1	2	3	4

3. Teachers or students can arrange to deviate from the prescribed program of the school.

4. The principal encourages experimentation in teaching.

5. Teachers are held accountable in this school for providing learning opportunities for each of their students.

Effective Teaching-Learning Strategies:

1. The teachers in this school know *how* to teach as well as what to teach.

2. When one teaching strategy does not seem to be working for a particular student, the teacher tries another; does not blame the student for the initial failure.

3. This community supports new and innovative teaching techniques.

4. Inservice education programs available to teachers in this building help them keep up-to-date on the best teaching strategies.

5. The school systematically encourages students to help other students with their learning activities.

Ability to Plan for the Future:

1. In this school we keep "looking ahead;" we don't spend all our time "putting out fires."

2. Our principal is an "idea" man.

	What Is:				What Should Be:			
Part C **Process Determinants** **(Continued)**	Almost Never	Occasionally	Frequently	Almost Always	Almost Never	Occasionally	Frequently	Almost Always
	1	2	3	4	1	2	3	4
3. Parents and community leaders have opportunities to work with school officials at least once a year on "things we'd like to see happening in our school."								
4. Some of the programs in our school are termed "experimental."								
5. Our school is ahead of the times.								

The CFK Ltd. School Climate Profile
Copyright 1973

(This instrument is part of an extensive description and analysis of the school's climate and should be used in association with *School Climate Improvement: A Challenge for the School Administrator.*)

I am a:
___Student
___Teacher
___Parent
___Secretary, custodian, or other staff member
___Administrator in this school
___Superintendent or central administrator

	What Is:				What Should Be:			
Part D **Material Determinants**	Almost Never	Occasionally	Frequently	Almost Always	Almost Never	Occasionally	Frequently	Almost Always
	1	2	3	4	1	2	3	4

Adequate Resources:

1. There is sufficient staff in this school to meet the needs of its students.

2. The instructional materials are adequate for our school program.

3. Curriculum materials used in this school give appropriate emphasis and accurate facts regarding ethnic and minority groups, and sex roles.

4. Resources are provided so that students may take advantage of learning opportunities in the community through field trips, work-study arrangements, and the like.

5. Current teacher salaries in this community give fair recognition of the level of professional service rendered by teachers to the community.

	What Is:				What Should Be:			
Part D **Material Determinants** **(Continued)**	Almost Never	Occasionally	Frequently	Almost Always	Almost Never	Occasionally	Frequently	Almost Always
	1	2	3	4	1	2	3	4

Supportive and Efficient Logistical System:

1. Teachers and students are able to get the instructional materials they need at the time they are needed.
2. Budget making for this school provides opportunities for teachers to recommend and make judgments about priorities for resources needed in their program.
3. The support system of this school fosters creative and effective teaching/learning opportunities rather than hinders them.
4. Necessary materials, supplies, etc., for learning experiences are readily available as needed.
5. Simple non-time-consuming procedures exist for the acquisition and use of resources.

Suitability of School Plant:

1. It is pleasant to be in this building; it is kept clean and in good repair.
2. This school building has the space and physical arrangements needed to conduct the kinds of programs we have.
3. Students and staff are proud of their school plant and help to keep it attractive.
4. The grounds are attractive and provide adequate space for physical and recreational activities.
5. Current teacher salaries in this community give fair recognition of the level of professional service by teachers to the community.

Directions for Summarizing Data on the
CFK Ltd. School Climate Profile

1. Separate questionnaires by role group.

2. Compute sum of ratings given by each individual respondent for each category. Since there are five items per category the maximum score could be twenty; the minimum score would be five, if the respondent had checked "1" "almost never," for each of the five items.

3. Write this score in the box provided after item five in each category, both for "What Is" and for "What Should Be."

4. Since there is more than one respondent for each role group, compute the mean score for each category by adding all the scores for each category and dividing by the number of respondents.

For example, suppose there are nine teacher questionnaires. Their scores on the General Climate Factor of "Respect" are as follows:*

Teacher	"What Is" Score	"What Should Be" Score
1	15	19
2	13	20
3	18	20
4	18	20
5	11	18
6	17	20
7	14	20
8	12	19
9	15	19
	9/133	9/175
	14.8	19.4

5. Plot these mean scores (14.8 and 19.4) on the summary form.

6. After computing in a similar manner the mean score for other climate factors, connect the "What Is" scores with a black line; connect "What Should Be" scores with a red line, or a broken line (---).

---

*See page 72 for example of plotting these scores on the summary form.

7. Use a different summary form for each role group.

8. Later you may want to compare responses of particular role groups by plotting them on the same summary form, or by converting the summary into a transparency and superimposing the data for the two role groups one on the other.

9. Summary Form of the CFK Ltd. School Climate Profile

It may be helpful to summarize the data from all the questionnaires into one summary form. This can give a total picture of the school's climate. So that the total picture is not distorted by including the results of 1,000 student questionnaires combined with five administrators and fifty teachers, it is recommended that the summary form be created from an averaging of the mean scores of each of the role groups, as follows:

Given the data shown on the summary forms for each of the six role groups, simply find the mean score on each climate item. For example, regarding the General Climate Factor of "Respect," let's assume the summary forms show scores on "What Is" as follows:

	Mean "What Is" Scores
Summary Form	
A. Students	12.2
B. Teachers	15.4
C. Parents	12.3
D. Other staff	15.0
E. Administrators	18.0
F. Central administrators	17.2
	$6/\overline{90.1}$
	$\overline{15.0}$

This mean score of 15.0 for "What Is" with regard to "Respect" would then be plotted on the summary form.

Summary Form of the CFK Ltd.
School Climate Profile

For _____ School

Based on data summarized from _____ respondents.
(State Role Group)

	Almost Never	Occasionally	Frequently	Almost Always
	5	10	15	20

A. GENERAL CLIMATE FACTORS
   1. Respect
   2. Trust
   3. High Morale
   4. Opportunities for Input
   5. Continuous Academic and
      Social Growth
   6. Cohesiveness
   7. School Renewal
   8. Caring

B. PROGRAM DETERMINANTS
   1. Opportunities for Active
      Learning
   2. Individualized Performance
      Expectations
   3. Varied Learning Environments
   4. Flexible Curriculum and
      Extracurricular Activities
   5. Support and Structure Appro-
      priate to Learner's Maturity
   6. Rules Cooperatively
      Determined
   7. Varied Reward Systems

C. PROCESS DETERMINANTS
   1. Problem-Solving Ability
   2. Improvement of School Goals
   3. Identifying and Working
      with Conflicts
   4. Effective Communications
   5. Involvement in Decision
      Making
   6. Autonomy with Accountability
   7. Effective Teaching-Learning
      Strategies
   8. Ability to Plan for the
      Future

D. MATERIAL DETERMINANTS
   1. Adequate Resources
   2. Supportive and Efficient
      Logistical System
   3. Suitability of School Plant

Summary Form of the CFK Ltd.
School Climate Profile

For _____ School

Based on data summarized from _____ respondents.
(State Role Group)

	Almost Never	Occasionally	Frequently	Almost Always
	5	10	15	20

A. GENERAL CLIMATE FACTORS
  1. Respect
  2. Trust
  3. High Morale
  4. Opportunities for Input
  5. Continuous Academic and
    Social Growth
  6. Cohesiveness
  7. School Renewal
  8. Caring

B. PROGRAM DETERMINANTS
  1. Opportunities for Active
    Learning
  2. Individualized Performance
    Expectations
  3. Varied Learning Environments
  4. Flexible Curriculum and
    Extracurricular Activities
  5. Support and Structure Appro-
    priate to Learner's Maturity
  6. Rules Cooperatively
    Determined
  7. Varied Reward Systems

C. PROCESS DETERMINANTS
  1. Problem-Solving Ability
  2. Improvement of School Goals
  3. Identifying and Working
    with Conflicts
  4. Effective Communications
  5. Involvement in Decision
    Making
  6. Autonomy with Accountability
  7. Effective Teaching-Learning
    Strategies
  8. Ability to Plan for the
    Future

D. MATERIAL DETERMINANTS
  1. Adequate Resources
  2. Supportive and Efficient
    Logistical System
  3. Suitability of School Plant

CHAPTER VI

School Climate Determinants

In this chapter, each of the contributing school climate determinants described earlier is detailed. In addition, indicators are provided that are designed to give the reader a picture of what each determinant might look like in a school where the climate for that particular determinant is exemplary.

Program Determinants

OPPORTUNITIES FOR ACTIVE LEARNING. When students are provided opportunities for active learning, they become totally involved in the learning process, both physically and mentally. Learning activities are designed to encourage students to carry through to some kind of action. Students are able to demonstrate an ability to utilize their knowledge and skills.

Some indicators of active learning include:

Individual interaction.

Group interaction.

Inquiry modes of learning.

Students are involved in determining their own needs and in planning their own program.

There is provision for student learning opportunities outside the school.

Opportunities are provided for career learning experiences that may become lifetime pursuits.

How this might be visible in:

Principal and other administrators

Have worked with staff and students on active learning opportunities in the school and community.

Share ideas, and provide support for teachers.

Provide for staff's continuous evaluation and feedback regarding opportunities for active learning.

Students

Feel the curriculum they are pursuing encourages them to be participants in the learning process.

Believe they can initiate activities for their learning either inside or outside the school.

Know there is someone they can interact with regarding any learning problem.

Are given opportunities for helping others in school and community.

Regularly interact with teachers to design individual learning activities.

Staff

Feels supported in efforts to provide active learning opportunities.

Practices active learning experiences for students as opposed to strictly lecture methods.

Continually searches for new approaches to active learning opportunities inside and outside the school.

Involves parents and community in designing curriculum learning activities.

Parents

Talk about the school and active learning opportunities in a positive and supportive manner.

Support active learning experiences in the home.

Have opportunities to help select the active learning programs for their children in the school and community.

INDIVIDUALIZED PERFORMANCE EXPECTATIONS.
They are reasonable, flexible, and make allowances for personalized performance expectations, since all individuals are different. That is, different standards of expectations are anticipated and rewarded. (Unfortunately, many schools are functioning as if there are predetermined academic, social, and physical standards for all children.) Individuals frequently are encouraged to set their own performance goals.

Because expectations differ, there may be a tendency to accept less than maximum performance. Care must be taken to allow for differences, while at the same time providing maximum challenges for fully motivating the individual.

If the program is to be personalized, the school must be able to diagnose the entry point of the individual and to plan collaboratively those activities that are stimulating, obtainable, and relevant.

How this might be visible in:

Principal and other administrators

Are supportive of individualized expectations.

Participate with other members of the educational community to work on and expand competencies necessary to personalized expectations.

Work to keep current with skills needed to individualize instruction.

Students

Are generally in competition with themselves rather than with each other.

Believe they have adults who will listen to their requests for personalized instruction programs and objectives.

Are able to identify their own strengths and weaknesses.

Staff

Has the competencies for diagnosing needs of students.

Establishes reasonable, but not overwhelming expectations.

Works together to identify and learn new skills for implementing individualized programs.

Will encourage students to generate their own game-plan for learning.

Parents

Are knowledgeable and supportive of different expectations for different children, including their own.

Believe the programs in the schools accommodate their (the parents') interests.

Share information with the school so they can establish realistic expectations for their children.

Will communicate freely with staff and students about expectations.

VARIED LEARNING ENVIRONMENTS. These are provided by the school for students and for educators. There is no one standard mode of instruction (such as the lecture method), class size, or atmosphere. The environment stimulates both students and staff to interact in an open and congenial way. Schools within schools and alternative programming are considered as potential processes for developing optional environments. Students are given the skills and tools to seek information on their own. Students can pursue their ideas independently, utilize teachers as resource tools in a manner similar to the way they utilize books, libraries, films, tapes, and other resources. Help is available not only from teachers, but from other staff, students, and other community members. The learning environment is not limited to the confines of the school building, but extends into the community. The students' programs are not limited to or by the physical environment and schedules.

How this might be visible in:

Principal and other administrators

See alternative schools as useful.

Recognize many kinds of learning environments both within and outside the school.

Make efforts to break up the large school into smaller, more face-to-face collegial groups.

Support variety rather than conformity.

Provide specialized environments for atypical children (but seldom in a manner to exclude them from contact with the rest of the school).

Students

Feel they can change their learning environment if need be.

Know service to others provides another type of learning—giving rather than getting.

Staff

Is comfortable in allowing students a freedom of choice.

Respects and encourages different styles and approaches.

Provides learning options appropriate to students' varying levels of maturity.

Parents

Feel they can select for their children from the varied learning environments those consistent with their own values and life styles.

Have a tolerance for diversity—do not insist that the environment they deem appropriate for their child should be imposed on all.

Have learning opportunities provided in the community as well as in the school.

Are utilized for learning as community resource people.

Are used as volunteers (retirees, nonemployed adults, mothers) to enrich learning.

Feel learning takes place in all parts of the learner's life space (some not under control of the school).

FLEXIBLE CURRICULUM AND EXTRACURRICULAR ACTIVITIES. These provide a wide variety of pace and content options for learners. It is not assumed all learners in a group have the same content needs or that most will learn at the same rate. Extracurricular activities serve all students and are subject to constant redevelopment as students' needs change. To the greatest extent possible, such activities are offered on an open-enrollment basis.

Formal opportunities are provided for all in the school to participate in curriculum and extracurricular programs. In this situation teachers, students, parents, administrators, and all connected with the school view the school as a learning experience to meet the needs of each student.

How this might be visible in:

Principal and other administrators, students, staff, and parents

Students have a wide variety of opportunities to succeed in academic, vocational, and personal interest areas, both inside and outside the school.

Programs that lead to graduation are tailored to the needs of the students.

There is a continual assessment, restructuring, and adjustment of all offerings and activities in keeping with the needs, interests, and paces of individual students. (The community, parents, professional educators, as well as the students, are involved in determining program direction.)

Programs provide opportunities for different entry levels and for short-term learning experiences (many courses) and in-depth experiences (full quarter), contracts, cooperatively planned units, independent projects, etc.

Opportunities for extracurricular learning experiences are provided throughout the school year.

Attempts are made to utilize all available community resources, both human and physical, in expanding and enhancing the educational opportunities for students.

Provision is made for implementation of programs appropriate for ethnic and minority groups.

SUPPORT AND STRUCTURE APPROPRIATE TO LEARNER'S MATURITY. The goal of the school is to design its programs, activities, and requirements so they are consistent with the ever-changing intellectual, social, and physical development characteristics of youth as they grow during childhood and adolescence. Thus, a necessary first requirement of this climate determinant is that elementary and secondary school educators are knowledgeable of and practice the principles of child and adolescent growth and development.

How this might be visible in:

Principal and other administrators:

Are alert to reducing structure as students mature.

Insure that students are not placed in situations that require abilities beyond their level of maturity.

Provide leadership in the school's efforts to design its programs to achieve consistency with knowledge of child and adolescent growth and development.

Students

Are able to take initiative to modify degree of structure.

Assist other students of different levels of maturity.

Staff

Provides a balance between freedom and structure appropriate to the learner's maturity.

Provides opportunities for students to practice self-discipline and responsibility.

Parents

Understand school's program for providing for students of different age levels differing balances between student freedom and structure.

RULES COOPERATIVELY DETERMINED. The process of developing school rules and regulations involves educators and students. They are clearly stated and viewed as reasonable and desirable by all. The rules for student behavior are most often determined by tradition and are rarely examined or updated. It is not unusual, for example, that a school with twenty outside portable classrooms will retain a rule that students are not allowed to wear coats to class.

Rules not only need to be updated periodically, but should be determined by all who are affected by them; e.g., administrators, teachers, students, and parents. Rules must apply equally to all, and they must be enforced consistently by all.

An effective guideline for the development of rules is to consider the kinds of behavior expected of students. As examples, teachers (parents) are punctual, as they expect students to be; teachers (parents) treat students with dignity and respect, as they expect students to do, etc.

Some indicators of rules cooperatively determined include:

Student groups have opportunities to develop the rules of the school.

Parents have opportunities to develop the rules of the school.

The staff has opportunities to develop the rules of the school.

The school rules are briefly stated and are limited to those kinds of behavior that promote student growth and development.

Students have a better understanding of and a greater commitment to the rules of the school.

Teachers and staff model the kinds of behavior that is expected of students.

VARIED REWARD SYSTEMS. Experiences are provided that help students and staff attain "ego" needs. Students are helped to develop personal identity and are provided with opportunities for growth, achievement, responsibility, and recognition. Skill development, competencies, and attitudes are important; grades are not of prime importance. The school minimizes punishment and emphasizes positive reinforcement of effective behavior.

A varied reward system is based upon the belief that success is good for students in their quest for self-actualization and that learning to fail is destructive. The school recognizes the need for and provides a wide variety of ways in which students and educators can be productive and successful. It eliminates demeaning activities, standard expectations and assumptions.

How this might be visible in:

Principal and other administrators
Believe in the need for students to succeed.

Encourage and support creative rewards for students.

Students
Feel that they have numerous opportunities to succeed.

Are supportive of the efforts of other students.

Are awarded credit for work accomplished.

Staff
Believes in the need for students to succeed.

Actively works towards the elimination of failure.

Recognizes that failure grades are demeaning and valueless.

Awards credit for work accomplished by individual students.

Parents

Feel that the school provides meaningful and supportive learning experiences for their children.

Provide positive feedback to teachers regarding class activities.

Process Determinants

PROBLEM-SOLVING ABILITY. In a school or school system where problem-solving skills are adequate, problems are solved with minimal energy. They stay solved, and the problem-solving mechanisms are maintained and strengthened. The organization has well-developed structures and procedures for sensing the existence of problems, for inventing possible solutions, for implementing them, and for evaluating their effectiveness. Problem-solving processes are evaluated and altered through experiences to increase their effectiveness.

How this might be visible in:

Principal and other administrators, students, staff, and parents

Every member of the school community works to identify and define problems or weaknesses, and honestly seeks the best possible solutions.

Each member of the school community understands the organization's processes for problem solving.

Each member of the school community has an opportunity to propose alternative possible solutions to the problem and openly discuss these alternatives.

Each of those concerned with the problem has input into the decision regarding which solution is selected for implementation; likewise, they are involved in the implementation and evaluation process.

CONTINUOUS IMPROVEMENT OF SCHOOL GOALS. The school's goals are clearly stated and understood by students, parents, and educators. They serve as reference points for making decisions, organizing school improvement projects, and guiding day-to-day operations. Improvement of school goals is a cooperative task for faculty, students, administrators, and parents in accord with school district goals as established by the school board, as the official representative of society. Each year opportunities are designed for persons representing various opinions of the above groups to work on the job of refining and updating goals. Goal refinement is a continuous updating process whereby goals are established and recorded. Data are gathered as a means of monitoring success in achieving each goal, and feedback is provided on progress and the goal evaluation process. Individuals affected by goals should have the opportunity to participate in establishing them and in the evaluation process.

The purpose of the process of periodically improving and examining the school's goals is to:

Record each academic and climate goal the school is currently attempting to achieve.

Continually update the goals of the organization.

Assist staff, administrators, students, and parents in understanding the precise reasons that the school exists.

Develop reference points staff and administrators can use for making decisions, organizing school improvement projects, and guiding day-to-day school operations.

How this might be visible in:

Principal and other administrators

Provide members with written statement of philosophy and importance of the process of continuous goal setting for the organization and for individuals associated with the school.

Develop management objectives for their school, themselves as individuals, and in their personalized professional growth plans.

Students

Are given opportunity to develop goals reflecting their own needs, interests, and abilities as individuals.

Have opportunities to select from a number of learning experiences.

Are provided with opportunities to set priorities and establish short- and long-term goals for student organizations (student government, clubs, intramurals, etc.) and for rules, regulations, classroom stability limits, assembly options and behavior, disciplinary procedures, etc.

Staff

Establishes goals for members' personal evaluation and defines data-gathering and feedback processes. (Evaluation is based on mutually agreed criteria.)

Is provided with the time and opportunity to assist students, colleagues, and administrators in setting goals, monitoring progress, and participating in evaluation of goals for the purpose of establishing personal/professional growth plans, and developing school improvement.

Parents

Are involved in the goal-setting process.

Participate in total process of continuous improvement of school goals.

IDENTIFYING AND WORKING WITH CONFLICTS. This process is necessary in developing a favorable school climate. Conflict is natural; it occurs within individuals, between them, and between groups. Conflict is not in itself a problem. It becomes troublesome when it mounts up, is not faced, and is allowed to fester. In a favorable school climate, conflict is identified and worked on.

Conflict between individuals and groups can be analyzed as misunderstanding because of inaccurate communication, as value differences because of different philosophical beliefs, and differences of opinion about actions to take when faced with a particular problem.

Conflict is not viewed as threatening, but instead is accepted as a natural phenomenon. There is an organized, formal structure through which students, staff, administrators, and parents identify and work on intrapersonal, interpersonal, and intergroup conflicts.

How this might be visible in:

Principal and other administrators

Spend time discussing interpersonal hindrances to being an effective team.

Feel competent and confident to deal openly with conflict and apply conflict management skills whenever necessary.

Encourage staff, students, and parents to identify conflict situations and to initiate steps to resolve the conflicts.

Provide opportunities for learning conflict management skills.

Students

Have skills that enable them to analyze and resolve interpersonal conflicts.

Feel willing to resolve interpersonal conflicts and feel that staff members are willing to assist them.

Seek help from staff members in resolving conflicts.

Point out, individually or as groups, conflict situations to administrator and/or other staff members.

Receive skill training for conflict management.

Staff

Feels competent in identifying and dealing with conflicts and feels that administrator supports their efforts.

Seeks training in conflict management skills.

Requests third party facilitation when necessary.

Assists students in resolving conflicts.

Takes concerns to the source rather than verbalizing concerns with friends.

Parents

Feel that their concerns will be listened to and are willing to bring them to administrators.

Seek skill training and practice conflict management in their homes.

EFFECTIVE COMMUNICATIONS. This process enhances interpersonal relationships between staff, students, and parents—rather than causing alienation, isolation, misunderstanding, fear, and frustration. It is a multidimensional process, not restricted by hierarchies or other imposed or imaginary barriers. There is an emphasis on sharing and problem solving and a concern for purposeful listening and effective message sending.

People are willing to express feelings and ideas that may be contrary to those of other people. They are willing to listen and to understand the feelings and ideas of others, which may be contrary to their feelings and ideas. They are willing to express praise for the accomplishments of others. A feeling of trust exists among those associated with the school.

How this might be visible in:

Principal and other administrators

Are receptive to ideas of individuals who are not part of the team.

Feel no threat in contact and communication.

Provide opportunities for the expression of feelings and ideas in areas of potential disagreement.

Students

Know that their opinions, reactions, or ideas will be listened to and considered.

Interact with consideration for rights of others.

Provide opportunities for others to express feelings and ideas that may be contrary to their own.

Staff

Knows that its opinions will be listened to and considered.

Communicates freely with other staff subgroups and shares ideas and feelings.

Individuals solicit help from other staff members.

Provides opportunities for others to express feelings and ideas that may be contrary to their own.

Share in planning within departments or other common interest groups.

Parents

Feel comfortable expressing their feelings and ideas to the school or to individuals within the school.

Have opportunity to discuss openly their concerns and their perceptions of the school's strengths and weaknesses.

INVOLVEMENT IN DECISION MAKING. This is a need that is understood by individuals and groups in a positive school climate. Opportunity for involvement in improving the school exists for students, educators, interested parents, and others. The extent of participation is determined by the individual in keeping with the needs of the school.

Persons affected by a decision have the opportunity to provide input into that decision. Decisions are based upon pertinent information. It may be impossible to have all information before a decision is necessary. Formal processes for decision making are specified and understood by all. Attention is given to the issue: Who will make decisions about factors such as budget, personnel, curriculum, athletic program, dress codes, etc. A variety of decision-making modes is considered, depending on the type of decision being made, such as delegated authority, majority vote, negotiation, and confrontation. The principal actively seeks the involvement of individuals and groups. Involvement can take various forms. Persons included in decision making are accountable for their decisions; responsible for communicating to others the results of decisions. The decision-making process is reviewed periodically for effectiveness and efficiency.

How this might be visible in:

Principal and other administrators

Have faith in staff support of decisions once they have been made.

Provide information for decision making that may not be available to other members of the staff.

Provide training to others to help them learn decision-making skills.

Realize that some people may have more competence than they on some topics.

Students

Assume responsibility for supporting decisions they helped make.

Accept ideas from other students that may be contrary to their own.

Feel that student representation is fact, not fiction.

Believe the adults in their lives are concerned about their futures.

Staff

Accept responsibility for sharing decisions.

Help to design a decision-making model and understand its function.

Support the decisions they help to make.

Support and encourage a diversity of opinions by other staff members.

Realize that not all other staff members may wish to participate in all decisions.

Are open to input and actively solicit it from other individuals and groups.

Parents

Feel they have a mechanism for influencing decisions.

Accept the concept of alternative decisions for instances where children have different needs.

Support decisions once they have been made.

Are involved in the decision-making process.

Support divergent thinking.

Are frequently included where decisions about their children are necessary.

Are willing to serve on *ad hoc* groups with children, staff, and administration.

AUTONOMY WITH ACCOUNTABILITY. This characteristic balances, on the one hand, the freedom of being independent and self-governing, and on the other, accepting the necessity and desirability of being responsible and answerable for actions through reporting and explaining progress in achieving goals and objectives. This characteristic applies not only to the school as an organization, but also to students and staff as individuals and as working groups.

Following are some illustrative conditions of autonomy with

accountability. Each person accepts responsibility for his actions. Different persons take initiative and responsibility in organizing and conducting school improvement projects. Persons with responsibility for an aspect of the school's program accept a commitment for achieving and communicating with others the degree of quality attained. Freedom exists for selecting and using varied and educationally effective learning processes.

A balance between autonomy and accountability is sought despite the difficulty of achieving it. Individuals or groups who assume leadership in making decisions or operating programs accept accountability for their performances.

How this might be visible in:

Principal and other administrators

Each models accountability in regard to identified job targets.

Administrative team members develop individualized job descriptions and goals.

Students

Can be as active or inactive as they desire in regard to school-wide activities.

Feel responsible for their behavior.

Are aware how their behavior affects others, both as individuals and as groups.

Have various responsibility, freedom, and structure according to age level and individual ability to handle.

Staff

Accepts responsibility for each student's learning needs including development of basic skills.

Feels responsible for each student's behavior.

Accepts the accountability for achieving the curriculum, and documents successes and failures.

EFFECTIVE TEACHING-LEARNING STRATEGIES. A school that employs effective teaching-learning strategies may be characterized by the following general indicators:

The specific goals for a given teaching-learning situation are clearly stated, and the teachers involved in that activity actively seek evaluative feedback from students and other educators.

Teachers recognize that students have a variety of learning styles and attempt to employ teaching methods that take into account learning styles as well as the learner's maturity.

Students have an understanding of various learning styles and teaching methods and have an opportunity to choose from the variety of learning activities.

Among students, inquiry is encouraged and student emphasis is placed on the learner's involvement in any activity.

Both parents and students have an understanding of the various learning activities available and have an opportunity to work with the teachers in designing each student's program.

A formal system exists to insure continuous evaluation and redesign of the teaching strategies used.

ABILITY TO PLAN FOR THE FUTURE. It is through planning processes that the school can determine its long-range future. Without an ability to act, to rationally and deliberately plan necessary and desirable school improvements, the school "drifts" into the future largely by the process of reacting. As such, the school—educators and clientele—can merely react to crises, complaints, and the latest fashionable innovation, which may or may not be of value to the particular school. When the school's and the school district's educators and clientele plan for the future, they tend to reduce the number of problems the school faces through the process of anticipating and planning desirable changes. The ability to plan for the future is a combination of isolating the school's "Images of Potentiality" (see pages 40-44) and using planning process skills. Input to the process of planning the future includes:

Changes in the youth culture.

Changes in curriculum, teaching-learning strategies, and in the school's role in the general society and local community.

Literary and other commentaries that present innovations advocated for schooling.

In short, dreams for the future are probably not going to occur unless they are translated into action. The planning process represents the vehicle for translating ideas into school improvement projects.

Some indicators of the ability to plan for the future include:

The school's educators assume a future orientation. They attempt to project conditions as they wish them to be.

The school's educators assume a school improvement project planning attitude. That is, they have some clear models as to how they are going to proceed to a decision from criteria, evidence to be collected, alternatives that are to be generated and analyzed, and those who should be involved in making judgments about the evidence and the alternatives.

The faculty and staff maintain an optimistic, open attitude exemplified by the acceptance of opinions and the reluctance to close upon a decision until the majority, if not all members, has had an opportunity to influence the final decision.

They assume a presumptive attitude. (If we can reach a decision about what is appropriate and commit ourselves to it, we can in some way find the human and material resources to accomplish the task.)

Material Determinants

ADEQUATE RESOURCES. The school secures able educators and supports them and students by providing quality resources including instructional material centers and laboratories, desirable classroom or learning area equipment, furniture, textbooks, other references, materials, and adequate expendable supplies.

Some indicators of adequate resources include:

Only rarely do educators and students have to modify learning activities due to inability to obtain resources that should commonly be available.

There are sufficient educators and staff members in the school to meet student needs.

The school's instructional materials and classroom facilities are appropriate for the school's program.

Resources are provided so that students may take advantage of action learning opportunities in the community through field trips, work-study arrangements, and the like.

SUPPORTIVE AND EFFICIENT LOGISTICAL SYSTEM.
The school's system provides varied services and resources to help people to be productive in achieving individual student and educator goals and the school's and school district's goals for its curriculum and extracurricular activities.

A supportive and efficient logistical system consists of the school's and school district's designed program and ability to effectively:

Secure able human resources (faculty, administrators, staff). Support educators, students, and staff members by providing quality resources including instructional material centers and laboratories; desirable classroom or learning area equipment, furniture, textbooks, other references, and materials; and adequate expendable supplies.

Obtain commonly used resources rapidly with an absence of inefficient procedures and delays.

Aid people by providing quality services in the areas of student scheduling, custodial, maintenance, secretarial, purchasing, budgeting, and accounting.

Modify the physical plant as program and human needs change.

Keep the building decor attractive through use of color, furniture arrangement, and displays of student work.

Conduct a straightforward communication program concerning what educators and citizens can and cannot expect of the school's logistical system. (Thus, help people to perceive the logistical system as it actually is.)

In all, the logistical system is designed to help people be productive in achieving the school's and school district's curriculum for each subject area, experience, and extracurricular activity. A responsive system enhances morale.

People with unique logistical responsibilities (custodians, secretaries, maintenance workers, purchasing agents, etc.) often receive appreciation from those served.

How this might be visible in:

Principal and other administrators

Administrative team does *not* feel burdened with logistical problems.

It is not necessary for administrative team members to spend inordinate amounts of time on logistics problems.

Administrators periodically conduct a survey to isolate logistics problems and monitor effectiveness of the system.

Students

When asked to list school concerns, logistical problems are not listed.

Necessary materials, supplies, etc., for learning experiences are readily available as needed.

Staff

When asked to list school concerns, logistical problems are not listed.

An understanding of the logistics system and common problems exists.

Working units of people or departments insure that the available logistical resources are equally distributed according to program needs.

Teachers do not have to modify learning activities due to inability to obtain resources that should commonly be available.

Simple rapid procedures exist for the acquisition or use of resources.

SUITABILITY OF SCHOOL PLANT. Students and employees of the school and school district modify the physical plant as program and human needs change. They keep the school's decor attractive through use of color, furniture arrangements, and displays of student work.

Some indicators of suitability of school plant are:

It is pleasant to be in the school building.

The building has appropriate space and physical arrangements needed to conduct its programs.

Students and staff are proud of their school plant and help keep it attractive.

The grounds are attractive, and provide adequate space for physical and recreational activities.

The school is kept clean and in good repair.

CHAPTER VII

How to Develop Indicators to Describe Climate Standards for Your School

The school climate descriptions and specific indicators of Chapters V and VI are a result of input from school staffs and administrators presently working on school climate improvement programs. This exercise can be used for any of the following purposes.

There may be great value, however, for each school to involve its own people in defining specifically what each of the climate determinants means to them, and in creating their own illustrations of the behaviors on the part of students, staff, administration, and parents that are good indicators. Procedures for doing this are described in this section.

Such an exercise might accomplish one or more of the following purposes:

1. To provide a quick reference as to what the determinant means and what it would look like in a school.

2. To assist a team of teachers, administrators, students, and/ or parents to develop a picture of what one or more of the determinants should look like in a particular school. This exercise can facilitate understanding.

3. To determine school climate improvement goals and strate-

gies by comparing "what is" and "what should be" as determined by the results of the CFK Ltd. School Climate Profile.

4. To develop one's own school climate assessment instrument or to modify the CFK Ltd. School Climate Profile by adding items of unique significance to one's school.

5. To develop an in-depth assessment instrument for one or a few of the school climate factors and determinants identified in Chapter I of this book. For example, assume one has used the CFK Ltd. School Climate Profile as is or as modified and, as a result, determined that three climate determinants appear to be weaknesses at his school. However, one desires to obtain further information by developing a survey instrument of greater depth and breadth.

This exercise will help the user achieve any of the above goals.

1. For each climate factor or determinant for which further work is needed, organize a brainstorming-writing team of three to seven members.

2. In recording their ideas, ask each team to use the worksheets that appear below. (Note: So as to provide more writing space for your teams, transfer the worksheets to "butcher" paper, legal-size paper, or multiple pages of 8½ x 11 sheets.)

3. Use the results of this work to achieve whichever of the above goals is sought.

Blank worksheets are provided here. Two examples of completed worksheets appear on pages 97 through 101.

SCHOOL CLIMATE FACTOR OR DETERMINANT:

Definition: (In the space below, briefly describe or define this school climate factor or determinant.)

Indicators: (Using the grid below, develop indicators for the school using this question: What does this factor or determinant look like in a quality school climate?)

Desirable Climate for	Collegial or Peer Relationships	Perceptions or Feelings of Individuals	Relationships among People with Different Role Responsibilities
Students			
Faculty and Staff			
Principal and Other Administrators			
Parents and School Community			

SCHOOL CLIMATE FACTOR OR DETERMINANT: Support and Structure Appropriate to Learner's Maturity

Definition: In this climate area, the goal of the school is to design its programs, activities, and requirements so they are consistent with the ever-changing intellectual, social, and physical development characteristics of youth as they grow during childhood and adolescence. Thus, a necessary first requirement of this climate element is that elementary and secondary school educators are knowledgeable of and practice the principles of child and adolescent growth and development.

In accord with such knowledge of students at different ages and stages of development, throughout its programs and activities, other requirements of an effective school are:

The school provides a balance between freedom and structure appropriate to learner's maturity.

On a planned basis, the school provides opportunities for students to practice self-discipline and responsibility.

While each student possesses a different rate of intellectual, social, and physical maturation, in general, to account for development differences, the school designs different programs. For example, different structures exist for seventh graders than for ninth graders, and structures are carefully designed for different age levels.

The school provides cross-age situations where students can assist other students at different maturity levels.

As students mature, the school is alert to reducing structure.

The school does not place students in situations that require abilities beyond their level of maturity.

Indicators:

Desirable Climate for	Collegial or Peer Relationships	Perceptions or Feelings of Individuals	Relationships among People with Different Role Responsibilities
Students		Feel challenged, not threatened or confined. Can take initiative to modify their degree of structure. Structure is not a bad word; the amount of structure for students changes in regard to learner's needs, readiness, and maturity.	Schedule and structure does not demand same amount of freedom and structure for each student. Program of extracurricular activities appropriate for age levels served.
Faculty and Staff	Professionals are able to practice knowledge of adolescent growth and development. Initiative is taken to discover maturity status of students; status is not assumed.	Structure is not a bad word; the amount of structure for students changes in regard to learner's needs, readiness, and maturity.	School provides opportunities for readiness for learning situations. Schedule and structure do not demand same amount of freedom and structure for each student. Program of extracurricular activities appropriate for age levels served.

Indicators:

Desirable Climate for	Collegial or Peer Relationships	Perceptions or Feelings of Individuals	Relationships among People with Different Role Responsibilities
Principal and Other Administrators	Principal assumes leadership in the school's efforts to design its programs to achieve consistency with knowledge of child and adolescent growth and development. Professionals are able to practice knowledge of adolescent growth and development. Initiative is taken to discover maturity status of students; status is not assumed.	Structure is not a bad word; the amount of structure for students changes in regard to learner's needs, readiness, and maturity.	Schedule and structure do not demand same amount of freedom and structure for each student. Program of extracurricular activities appropriate for age levels served.
Parents and School Community		Parents understand school's program for providing differing balances between student freedom and structure for different age levels of students.	Schedule and structure do not demand same amount of freedom and structure for each student. Program of extracurricular activities appropriate for age levels served.

SCHOOL CLIMATE FACTOR OR DETERMINANT: Varied Learning Environments

Definition: Varied learning environments employ methods of learning other than the teacher lecture method. The environment stimulates both student and staff to interact in an open and congenial way. Students are given the skills and tools to seek information on their own. Students with strong self-actualization move to pursue their ideas independently, utilize teachers as resource tools in a manner similar to the way they utilize books, libraries, films, tapes, and expertise. The environment involves small-group sessions, large-group sessions, one-to-one contacts, and self-study. In addition, it assists students who are not capable of self-actualization methods. Help is available not only from teachers, but also from other staff, students, and other community members. The learning environment is not limited to the confines of the school building, but extends into the community at large. The students' program is not limited to and by the physical environment or schedule.

Indicators:

Desirable Climate for	Collegial or Peer Relationships	Perceptions or Feelings of Individuals	Relationships among People with Different Role Responsibilities
Students	Would interact openly and freely with each other in a variety of learning situations. Service to others provides another type of learning—giving rather than getting. Students would recognize and respect their different levels of ability.	The student feels he can change his learning environment if need be. He feels his own interests can be pursued. The student feels comfortable in making decisions to pursue his choice.	It is acceptable to have both teacher-directed and student-directed learning options. Students are delighted, on occasion, to be able to teach their teachers when they have some specialized skill or knowledge.

Indicators:

Desirable Climate for	Collegial or Peer Relationships	Perceptions or Feelings of Individuals	Relationships among People with Different Role Responsibilities
Faculty and Staff	Special strengths of staff members are capitalized upon. Teachers share good ideas they may be trying out in their classrooms. Teachers respect and encourage different styles and approaches.	Are comfortable in allowing students a freedom of choice. Faculty and staff are active in teaching skills and tools of learning to students. Faculty and staff move to facilitate a catalytic role.	Learning options are provided appropriate to students' varying levels of maturity.
Principal and Other Administrators	Efforts are made to break up the large school into smaller, more face-to-face collegial groups. Principal supports variety, not conformity.	Alternative schools are seen as useful, not threatening. Administrators recognize that some kinds of learning environments are unacceptable to school.	Specialized environments are provided for atypical children (but seldom in a manner to exclude them from contact with the rest of the school).

Indicators:

Desirable Climate for	Collegial or Peer Relationships	Perceptions or Feelings of Individuals	Relationships among People with Different Role Responsibilities
Parents and School Community	Teacher aides are generally a part of the teaching team.	Parents feel they can select learning environments consistent with their own values and life style. Parents have a tolerance for diversity—do not insist that the environment they deem appropriate for their child should be imposed on all.	Learning opportunities are provided in the community as well as in the school. Community resource people are utilized for learning. Volunteers (retirees, nonemployed adults, mothers) are used in the school to enrich learning. Learning takes place in all parts of the learner's life space (some not under control of the school).

Pool of Items for School Climate Profile Instruments

The preceding section suggests that one goal might be to develop a climate assessment instrument for the school, to adapt the CFK Ltd. School Climate Profile, or to develop an in-depth instrument for one or more of the climate factors or determinants. Further, it was suggested that using the foregoing grid worksheets will be of assistance.

Eventually, a pool of highly relevant survey items for the school will emerge.

The following provides a beginning designed to assist in developing a pool of items for school climate assessment instruments.

Program Determinants

OPPORTUNITIES FOR ACTIVE LEARNING:
1. Students are involved in determining their own needs and in planning their own program.
2. Students feel they can initiate activities for their own learning.
3. Students feel the curriculum is relevant to their needs.
4. Students feel they compete with themselves rather than with others.
5. Each student feels he can consult at least one person regarding his learning.
6. Students have skills to work together on designing, developing, and implementing active learning activities.
7. The school's educators believe students' learning experiences outside school are as important as those inside.
8. The school's educators provide active learning experiences for students as opposed to strictly lecture methods.
9. The principal provides leadership for development of active learning opportunities throughout the school.
10. The school's educators continually search for new learning activities and revise and refine current activities.
11. The school's educators provide opportunities for student participation in curriculum development and design of learning activities.
12. The school's educators work with the community on active learning designs.
13. The school provides opportunities for students to learn outside the school.
14. The school provides opportunities for community members to teach within the school.
15. Parents feel they can contribute to the school's program if they so desire.
16. Parents work with the school to provide active learning experiences inside and outside the school environment.

17. Teachers, students, and administrators view themselves as active learners.

18.

19.

INDIVIDUALIZED PERFORMANCE EXPECTATIONS:

1. Students look upon their learning as being relevant to their immediate and long-range plans.

2. Students believe they are able to plan some of their own learning activities.

3. Students believe they have adults who will listen to their requests for personalized instruction programs and objectives.

4. Staff members have competencies for diagnosing needs of students.

5. Staff members have competencies to establish reasonable, but not overwhelming, expectations.

6. Staff members work with each other to identify and learn new skills for implementing individualized programs.

7. Staff members confer frequently with community groups to help keep communications open and expectations realistic.

8. The principal believes in individualized expectations.

9. The administrative team establishes different roles and responsibilities depending upon needs of the school on the one hand and competencies of team members on the other.

10. The administrative team works to keep current with skills needed to individualize instruction.

11. The administrative team participates with other members of the educational community to expand competencies necessary for personalized expectations.

12. Parents are knowledgeable and supportive of different expectations for different children including their own.

13. The school shares information with parents so they can establish realistic expectations for their children.

14. Parents communicate openly with staff and students about expectations.

15.

16.

VARIED LEARNING ENVIRONMENTS:

1. The student feels he can change his learning environment if need be.

2. The student feels his own interests can be pursued.

3. The student feels comfortable in making decisions to pursue his own choices.

4. Students recognize and respect their different levels of interests.

5. It is acceptable to have both teacher-directed and student-directed learning options.

6. Students are delighted, on occasion, to be able to teach their teachers when they have some specialized skill or knowledge.

7. Faculty and staff are comfortable in allowing students alternatives.

8. Faculty and staff are active in teaching learning skills and tools.

9. Learning options are provided appropriate to varying levels of maturity.

10. Alternative programs are seen as useful, not threatening.

11. Efforts are made to break up the large school into smaller, more face-to-face collegial groups.

12. The principal supports variety, not conformity.

13. Specialized environments are provided for atypical children (but seldom in a manner to exclude them from contact with the rest of the school).

14. Parents have a tolerance for diversity; they do not insist that the environment they deem appropriate for their child should be imposed on all.

15. Learning opportunities are provided in the community as well as in the school.

16. Community resource people are utilized for learning.
17. Volunteers (retirees, nonemployed adults, mothers) are used in the school to enrich learning.
18.
19.

FLEXIBLE CURRICULUM AND EXTRACURRICULAR ACTIVITIES:

1. Students have a wide variety of opportunities to succeed in academic, vocational, and personal interest areas both inside and outside the school.
2. All offerings and activities are continually assessed, restructured, and adjusted in keeping with the needs and interests of individual students. The community, parents, and professional educators, as well as the students, are involved in determining program direction.
3. Programs provide opportunities for different entry levels and for short-term learning experiences and in-depth experiences (full quarter), contracts, cooperatively planned units, independent projects, etc.
4. Attempts are made to utilize all available community resources, both human and physical, in expanding and enhancing the educational opportunities for students.
5. The school organizes a team of local community leaders to assist in identifying areas of need within the community where students can serve as volunteer workers.
6. The principal organizes a task force composed of parents, students, and teachers to design, organize, and staff a series of two-week mini-courses based on a recent student interest survey.
7. Formal opportunities are provided for all in the school to participate in curriculum development. In this situation teachers, students, parents, administrators, and all connected with the school should view the school as a learning organism in which all are learners.
8.
9.

SUPPORT AND STRUCTURE APPROPRIATE
TO LEARNER'S MATURITY:

1. The school designs its programs, activities, and requirements so that they are consistent with the ever-changing intellectual, social, and physical development characteristics of youth as they grow during childhood and adolescence.

2. Elementary and secondary school educators are knowledgeable of and practice the principles of child and adolescent growth and development.

3. The school provides a balance between freedom and structure appropriate to learners' maturity.

4. On a planned basis, the school provides opportunities for students to practice self-discipline and responsibility.

5. Because each student possesses a different rate of intellectual, social, and physical maturation, the school designs different programs to account for development differences. For example, different structures exist and are carefully designed for different age levels.

6. The school provides cross-age situations where students can assist other students at different maturity levels.

7. As students mature, the school is alert to reducing structure.

8. The school does not place students in situations that require abilities beyond their level of maturity.

9. Students can take initiative to modify their degree of structure.

10. Structure is not a bad word; the amount of structure for students changes in regard to learners' needs, readiness, and maturity.

11. Schedule and structure do not demand the same amount of freedom and structure for each student.

12. The program of extracurricular activities is appropriate for the age levels each program serves.

13. Professionals are able to practice their knowledge of adolescent growth and development.

14. Initiative is taken to discover the maturity status of

students; status is not assumed.

15. School provides opportunities for readiness for learning situations.

16. The principal assumes leadership in the school's efforts to design its programs to achieve consistency with knowledge of child and adolescent growth and development.

17. Parents understand the school's program for providing differing balances between student freedom and structure for different age levels of students.

18.

19.

VARIED REWARD SYSTEMS:

1. Success is good for students in their quest for self-actualization; learning to fail is destructive.

2. The school recognizes there are numerous ways one can be productive and successful.

3. Students feel that they have numerous opportunities to succeed.

4. Students are supportive of efforts of other students.

5. Failure grades are recognized as valueless and demeaning.

6. Students are awarded credit for work accomplished and not forced to adhere to nor restricted to a quarter or semester work.

7. Faculty and staff believe in the need for students to succeed.

8. Faculty and staff actively work towards the elimination of failure.

9. The school awards partial credits or increased credits for work accomplished.

10. Administrators encourage creative rewards for students.

11. Parents feel that the school provides meaningful and supportive learning experiences for their children.

12.

13.

RULES COOPERATIVELY DETERMINED:
1.
2.

Process Determinants

PROBLEM-SOLVING ABILITY:
1. Problems are solved with minimal energy. They stay solved, and the problem-solving mechanisms used are not weakened, but are maintained or strengthened.
2. The school has well-developed structures and procedures for sensing the existence of problems, for inventing possible solutions, for implementing them, and for evaluating their effectiveness.
3. Every member of the school community (students, teachers, parents, and administrators) works to identify and define problems or weaknesses, and honestly seeks the best possible solutions.
4. Problem-solving processes are themselves evaluated and altered through experiences to increase their effectiveness.
5. All members of the school community actively seek to identify problems and understand the school's processes for solving problems.
6. All members of the school community have an opportunity to propose alternative solutions to a problem and openly discuss these alternatives.
7. All those concerned with the problem have input into the decision regarding solutions; they are involved in the implementation and evaluation process.
8. Teachers recognize they are unable to achieve instructional goals through the lecture method alone and openly admit this.
9. Principal explores alternatives for delegating responsibility and lists the pros and cons of each approach.
10. Teachers model the types of problem-solving behaviors in their classroom and with fellow teachers they wish other faculty members to exhibit.

11. The principal models problem-solving skills.

12. The principal provides opportunity for inservice education to upgrade problem-solving skills.

13. Parents demonstrate a willingness to accept a consensus decision even though it may be contrary to personal views.

14.

15.

CONTINUOUS IMPROVEMENT OF SCHOOL GOALS:

1. The school publishes each academic and climate goal it is currently attempting to achieve.

2. The school continually updates the goals of the school.

3. School goals are designed to assist staff, administrators, students, and parents in understanding the precise reasons that particular school exists.

4. The school's goals are used as reference points that staff and administrators can use for making decisions, organizing school improvement projects, and guiding day-to-day school operations.

5. In accord with school district goals as established by the school board, as the official representative of society, the continuous improvement of the school's goals is a cooperative task for faculty, students, administrators, and parents.

6. Each year opportunities are designed for persons representing various shades of opinion to work on the job of refining and updating goals.

7. Goal refinement is a continuing, self-renewing process whereby goals are established, data are gathered as means of monitoring success in achieving each goal, and feedback is provided on progress and the goal evaluation process.

8. Individuals affected by goals should have the opportunity to participate in establishing them and in the evaluation process.

9. Because the greater majority of school goals inevitably

becomes the professional responsibility of teachers and administrators, they are heavily involved in the goal-setting process.

10. Goals reflecting need, interests, and abilities of individual students are reflected in overall program planning and in the program of each classroom.

11. Students have opportunities to select much of their program, in classroom activities to select from numerous learning experiences, and in classroom to design individualized learning or developmental tasks.

12. Student groups are provided with opportunities to set priorities and establish short- and long-term goals for student organizations (student government, clubs, intramurals, etc.) and for rules, regulations, classroom stability limits, assembly options and behavior, disciplinary procedures, etc.

13. Student groups have opportunity to participate in establishing and assessing school goals as they affect the total school and subgroups within the school.

14. Individual staff members establish goals for their personal evaluation, define data-gathering and feedback processes. Evaluation is based on mutually agreed criteria.

15. Teachers are provided with opportunities to participate in setting goals for the school, departments, etc., including curriculum direction, budget allocations, personal needs, and selection of new personnel.

16. Staff members are provided with the time and opportunity to assist students, colleagues, and administrators in setting goals, monitoring progress, and participating in evaluation of goals for the purpose of establishing personal/professional growth plans and developing school improvement projects.

17. The administration provides a written statement of philosophy and importance of the process of continuous goal setting for the organization and for individuals associated with the school.

18. Administrators have professional growth plan goals,

share them with others and receive feedback and evaluation from a wide range of staff members.

19. The administration develops management objectives for the school, themselves as individuals, and in their professional and personalized growth plans.

20. Parents participate in the total process of continuous improvement of school goals.

21. Citizens involved in school affairs can verbalize the value of continuous goal setting.

22. There is evidence of citizen satisfaction in the goal-setting process for the school district, the individual school, and each subject area.

23.

24.

IDENTIFYING AND WORKING WITH CONFLICTS:

1. Students are aware of conflicts within themselves in the way of productive learning and development and perceive they have opportunity to work on these conflicts; e.g., conflicts over work and play, and peer group values.

2. Students have a norm for pluralism of values within the peer group. They hold discussions about conflict between students (individuals and groups) and have organized opportunities to work on the conflicts.

3. Teachers and students discuss how interpersonal irritations might be hindering the classroom processes.

4. Students and educators give feedback to one another and use these opportunities to improve learning conditions.

5. Staff members hold a norm for pluralism of values within the staff.

6. Time is spent discussing the hindrances that are occurring in carrying out productive work as a staff.

7. Administrators and staff spend formal time identifying conflicts that are keeping the staff from being optimally effective; e.g., confusion over who makes what decision, etc.

8. Administrators are aware of conflicts between their controlling-authoritarian self and their humanistic-democratic self and perceive they have opportunity to work on these conflicts.

9. Administrators openly discuss their individual preferences for responsibilities.

10. Time is spent discussing interpersonal hindrances to being an effective administrative team.

11. The administrative team initiates sessions with subgroups of students, or central office personnel to discuss conflicts and to solve problems.

12. Parents get together with administration, teachers, and students to discuss tensions and concerns and to solve problems.

13. There is an organized formal structure through which students, staff, administrator, and parents can identify and work on conflicts.

14.

15.

EFFECTIVE COMMUNICATIONS:

1. Students know their opinions, reactions, or ideas will be listened to and considered.

2. Students interact with consideration for rights of others.

3. Students provide opportunities for others to express feelings and ideas that may be contrary to their own.

4. Faculty and staff know that their opinions will be listened to and considered.

5. The faculty and staff communicate freely with other staff subgroups and share ideas and feelings.

6. Individuals solicit help from other staff members.

7. Staff members provide opportunities for others to express feelings and ideas that may be contrary to their own.

8. The administrative team is receptive to ideas of individuals who are not part of the team.

9. The leadership team provides opportunities for the expression of feelings and ideas in areas of potential disagreement.

10. Parents feel comfortable expressing their feelings and ideas to the school or to individuals within the school.

11. Formal opportunity is available to parents to openly discuss their concerns and their perceptions of the school's strengths and weaknesses.

12. People are willing to express feelings and ideas that may be contrary to those of other people.

13. People are willing to listen and to understand the feelings and ideas of others.

14. People are willing to express praise for the accomplishments of others.

15. A feeling of trust exists among those associated with the school.

16.

17.

INVOLVEMENT IN DECISION MAKING:

1. Persons affected by a decision have opportunity to provide input into that decision.

2. Decisions are based upon pertinent information, but it may be impossible to have all information before a decision is necessary.

3. Formal processes for decision making are specified and understood by all.

4. A variety of decision-making modes is considered depending on the type of decision being made; e.g., delegated authority, majority vote, negotiation, confrontation.

5. The principal actively seeks the involvement of individuals and groups. Involvement can be at various levels.

6. Persons included in decision making are accountable for their decisions.

7. Persons responsible for making decisions have an obligation to communicate to others the results of decisions.

8. The decision-making process should be reviewed

9. Students believe they have a mechanism whereby their concerns can be aired and acted upon.

10. Students believe they are prepared in classes to analyze problems and to select solutions from among viable choices.

11. Students assume responsibility for supporting decisions they help make.

12. Students accept ideas from other students that may be contrary to their own.

13. Students believe that student representation is fact, not fiction.

14. Students feel they can openly participate with all other individuals in decision making.

15. Teachers consult with students prior to making decisions about instructional goals.

16. Students believe the adults in their lives are concerned about their futures.

17. Staff members are open to input and actively solicit it from other individuals and groups.

18. Students and parents are frequently represented on the curriculum study groups.

19. Staff members expect support from the principal, and, in turn, support the principal.

20. Staff members feel a responsibility for sharing decisions.

21. Staff members help design a decision-making model and understand its function.

22. Staff members support the decisions they help make.

23. Staff members support and encourage a diversity of opinions by other staff members.

24. Staff members realize that not all staff members may wish to participate in all decisions.

25. Staff members support each other when carrying out decisions.

26. The principal believes that decisions made collectively

are usually better than those made singly.

27. The principal believes that it is a right, not a privilege, to share in decisions.

28. The principal has faith in staff support of decisions once they have been made.

29. The principal provides training to others to help them learn decision-making skills.

30. The principal seeks formal and informal avenues for obtaining information before decisions are made.

31. The principal realizes that some people may have more competence than he on some topics.

32. The principal realizes shared decision making may require more time than other more traditional approaches to decision making.

33. Parents are frequently included where decisions about their children are necessary.

34. Parents are willing to serve on *ad hoc* groups with children, staff, and administration.

35. Parents support students, staff, and administration decisions where appropriate and try to change those decisions through reasonable routes where they believe the decisions are not viable.

36. The parents feel thay have a mechanism for influencing decisions.

37. Parents support decisions once they have been made.

38. The parents support divergent thinking.

39.

40.

AUTONOMY WITH ACCOUNTABILITY:

1. The school's programs and processes of education are constantly being improved.

2. Many different persons take initiative and responsibility in organizing and conducting school improvement projects.

3. Persons with responsibility for an aspect of the school's program accept a commitment for achieving and com-

municating with others the degree of quality attained.

4. Each individual has the freedom to choose his own behavior within the school—within the confines of the school's rules, which have been cooperatively determined.

5. The school's educators gain respect for their competencies as professionals and as humans. Freedom exists for selecting and using varied and educationally effective learning processes.

6. In regard to school-wide activities, each student can be as active or inactive as he desires.

7. Each student feels responsible for his behavior.

8. Individuals and groups are aware of how their behavior affects others.

9. Each student has the opportunity to select curriculum and extracurricular learning experiences appropriate to his needs and age level.

10. Responsibility, freedom, and structure for students varies according to age level and individual ability.

11. Learning experiences are differentiated to attract interest of varied student subpopulations.

12. Each faculty member accepts responsibility for each student's learning needs, including development of basic skills.

13. Each educator feels responsible for his behavior.

14. Faculty and staff examine the desirable balance between autonomy and accountability.

15. Prevailing norms are examined by faculty and staff to determine the extent to which they wish to be governed by them or vary from them.

16. Accountability for achieving the curriculum is accepted and success documented by faculty members.

17. Each administrator feels responsible for his behavior.

18. For benefit of students, faculty, and staff, each administrator models accountability in regard to identified job targets.

19. Principles drawn from knowledge of adolescent growth and development guide the school's operations.

20. Prevailing norms for administrators are examined to determine the extent to which they wish to be governed by them or vary from them.
21. The school district outlines necessary leadership services to be provided within each school.
22. Administrative team members develop individualized job descriptions and goals.
23. To enhance autonomy the kinds of decisions made are examined to achieve decentralization of decision making.
24. A balance between autonomy and accountability is sought, though perhaps never achieved.
25. Suggestions for school improvement from all possible sources are actively sought and considered.
26. Individuals or groups who assume leadership in making decisions or operating programs accept accountability for their performances.
27. Persons or groups with autonomy for the operation of programs and for arriving at decisions continually inform others about their endeavors.
28. An open school society exists. Persons feel there are no hidden barriers pertaining to age, race, cliques, sex, socio-economic conditions, hierarchy, etc., and, indeed, there are none.
29. If the school is a setting for learning, and if everything that is to occur is for the purpose of student growth, the right to fail exists.
30.
31.

EFFECTIVE TEACHING-LEARNING STRATEGIES:
1. The specific goals for a given teaching-learning situation are clearly stated, and the teachers involved in that activity actively seek evaluative feedback from students and peers.
2. Teachers recognize that students have a variety of learning styles and attempt to employ teaching methods

that take into account the learning style as well as the learner's maturity.

3. Students have an understanding of various learning styles and teaching methods and have an opportunity to choose from among the variety of learning activities.
4. Among students, inquiry is encouraged and student emphasis is placed on the learner's involvement in any activity.
5. Both parents and students have an understanding of the various learning activities available and have an opportunity to work with the teachers in designing each student's program.
6.
7.

ABILITY TO PLAN FOR THE FUTURE:
1. Parents, staff, and students are actively involved in planning future school improvements.
2. Planning models are being utilized by members of the planning teams.
3. Goals for future improvement are accepted by parents, staff, students.
4. Planning for the future is an integral part of the administrator's job role.
5.
6.

Material Determinants

ADEQUATE RESOURCES
1.
2.

SUPPORTIVE AND EFFICIENT LOGISTICAL SYSTEM:
1. People perceive the logistical system as it actually is.

2. The logistical system is designed to help people be productive in achieving the school's or school district's curriculum for each subject area, experience, and extracurricular activity.

3. A responsive logistical system enhances morale.

4. When asked to list school concerns, logistical problems are not listed by students.

5. Necessary materials, supplies, etc. for learning experiences are readily available as needed.

6. When asked to list school concerns, logistical problems are not listed by faculty and staff.

7. An understanding of logistics system and associated common problems exists.

8. Working units of people or departments insure that the available logistical resources are equally distributed according to program needs.

9. Teachers do not have to modify learning activities due to inability to obtain resources that should commonly be available.

10. Simple, rapid procedures exist for the acquisition or use of resources.

11. The administrative team does not feel burdened with logistical problems.

12. It is not necessary for administrative team members to spend inordinate amounts of time on logistics problems.

13. Periodically, administrators conduct a survey to isolate logistics problems and monitor effectiveness of the system.

14. A program exists to keep the building attractive.

15. People with unique logistical responsibilities (custodians, secretaries, maintenance repair workers, purchasing agents, etc.) often receive appreciation from those served.

16.

17.

SUITABILITY OF SCHOOL PLANT:

1. Plant contains no obvious safety hazards to students or staff.

2. Improvements to school plant that reflect staff and student needs are made on a regular basis.

3. The school program is designed to take advantage of the features of the school plant.

4. The school plant complements the unique capabilities of the staff.

5.

6.

CHAPTER VIII

Why Do It: Rationale for Organizing School Climate Improvement

This book focuses in part on the administrator's role in developing an improved humane school environment for learning. The administrator can be an effective and dynamic climate leader if he develops a participative climate that involves all who are part of the school environment, and some who are not.

In developing a rationale for organizing planned school climate improvement programs, the following concepts and opinions will be helpful to the administrator:

The concept of school climate improvement does not deemphasize skills, attitudes, and knowledge students gain through studies in academic areas such as language arts, social studies, mathematics, and science. It suggests that the most efficient learning programs occur in a wholesome and humane school climate.

School personnel can affect positively the nature and the wholesomeness of the school's climate. If it is inadequate, the fault rests with them, and the failure is a direct reflection upon the administrator as a climate leader.

School principals are not trapped by the existing conceptualization of their roles and by the accompanying expectations established for them by such factors as tradition, prevailing practice, faculty, parents, and students. The principal is a prisoner of these forces only if he lacks the strength and vision to create his own role. The following, from the study of change in the League of Cooperating Schools, is pertinent:

> The principal can be a key agent for change. However, even the best principals as rated by superintendents need a whole new set of skills in order to be effective change agents. These skills include such things as managing decision making; implementing scientific problem solving procedures; becoming aware of a great variety of resources which can be brought to bear on such problem solving; becoming more discriminating in selecting such resources; and developing the skills to deal with the conflict built in the middle management role.
>
> The principal as a change agent in effect becomes a "rate buster." That is, he differs from his fellow principals by setting higher goals for himself and his school.[1]

A United States Senate Select Committee presents this view of the principalship:

> In many ways the school principal is the most important and influential individual in any school. He is the person responsible for all the activities that occur in and around the school building. It is his leadership that sets the tone of the school, the climate for learning, the level of professionalism and morale of teachers and the degree of concern for what students may or may not become. He is the main link between the school and the community and the way he performs in that capacity largely determines the attitudes of students and parents about the school. If a school is a vibrant, innovative, child-centered place, if it has a reputation for excellence in teaching, if students are performing to the best of their ability, one can almost point to the principal's leadership as the key to success.
>
> We believe there is a need to revitalize the leadership role of school principals, reduce their administrative burdens and permit them to exercise the kind of responsibility necessary to make education work. At the same time, we believe if schools are to be more accountable to their clients, as the person most responsible for education where it happens, the principal should also be the person who is held accountable for the performance of the school, its teachers and students.[2]

Following are five views on school climate and environment.

School staffs are becoming increasingly aware that their professional work is done within an organizational and interpersonal climate. The climate is dependent upon such variables as:

Communication patterns.

Norms about what's appropriate or how things should be done.

Role relationships and role perceptions.

Influence relationships.

Rewards and sanctions.

There are two basic indicators of a healthy school climate: effective learning and personal satisfaction. In schools with healthy climates, innovations are easily developed and teachers feel good about their relationships. If the climate is not healthy, there may be low innovativeness, job dissatisfaction, alienation, lack of creativity, complacency, conformity, and frustration.[3]

What roles should the organized climate of the school play in developing constructive attitudes contributing to promoting the abilities and personal traits of all students? It is not enough that we answer this question or pursue this inquiry from the standpoint of general philosophy because it is in the school's practices that we give conscious or unconscious answers to every implication of this problem. It matters not how much we extol the promotion of an expanding student responsibility as one of the aims of the school if we hold mature students continually in the shadow of authority and require all to answer to regulations designed to trap the indifferent.[4]

There are two sections to almost every school's statement of educational objectives—one for real, and one for show. The first, the real one, talks about academic excellence, subject mastery, and getting into college or a job. The other discusses the humane purpose of the school—values, feelings, personal growth, the full and happy life. It is included because everyone knows that it is important, and that it ought to be central to the life of the school. But it is only for show. Everyone knows how little schools have done about it.[5]

The climate of an organization is the first and most important concern in initiating and sustaining change. People simply do not change in a threatening atmosphere—they become defensive and entrench. They may change surface behaviors—conform—receive and respond at the lowest level possible and acceptable to the powers that be; but attitudinal change and subsequent behavioral change must be preceded by perceptual change. This implies a willingness to accept new information. It is here that the stage for change is set.[6]

An administrator is powerful because he can marshall the necessary authority, if not the necessary leadership, to precipitate a decision. He may not be, and frequently is not, the original source of interest in a new type of program, but unless he gives it his attention and actively promotes its use, it will not come into being.[7]

John W. Gardner, former secretary of the U.S. Department of Health, Education, and Welfare, describes aspects of the leader's role. His comments pertain to the school administrator, among others.

If anything significant is to be accomplished, leaders must understand the social institutions and processes through which action is carried out. And in a society as complex as ours, that is no mean achievement.[8]

Most leaders are hedged around by constraints—tradition, constitutional limitations, the realities of the external situation, rights and privileges of followers, the requirements of teamwork, and most of all the inexorable demands of large-scale organization, which does not operate on capriciousness. In short, most power is wielded circumspectly. There are many different ways of leading, many kinds of leaders.[9]

Nothing should be allowed to impair the effectiveness and independence of our specialized leadership groups. But such fragmented leadership does create certain problems. One of them is that it isn't anybody's business to think about the big questions that cut across specialities—the largest questions facing our society. Where are we headed? Where do we WANT to head? What are the major trends determining our future? Should we do anything about them? Our fragmented leadership fails to deal effectively with these transcendent questions.[10]

For a good many academic and other professional people, negative attitudes toward leadership go deeper than skepticism concerning the leader's integrity. Many have real doubts, not always explicitly formulated, about the necessity for leadership.

The doubts are of two kinds. First, many scientific and professional people are accustomed to the kinds of problems that can be solved by expert technical advice or action. It is easy for them to imagine that any social enterprise could be managed in the same way. They envisage a world that does not need leaders, only experts. The notion is based, of course, upon a false conception of the leader's function. The supplying of technically correct solutions is the least of his responsibilities.

There is another kind of question that some academic or professional people raise concerning leadership: Is the very notion of leadership somehow at odds with the ideals of free society? It is a throwback to earlier notions of social organization?

These are not foolish questions. We have in fact outgrown or rejected several varieties of leadership that have loomed large in the history of mankind. We do not want autocratic leaders who treat us like inferior beings. We do not want leaders, no matter how wise or kind, who treat us like children. . . . our best leaders today are NOT out of place in a free society—on the contrary, they strengthen our free society.

We can have the kinds of leaders we want, but we cannot choose to do without them. . . . The sad truth is that a great many of our organizations are badly managed or badly led. And because of that, people within those organizations are frustrated when they need not be frustrated. They are not helped when they could be helped. They are not given the opportunities to fulfill themselves that are clearly possible.

In the minds of some, leadership is associated with goals that are distasteful—power, profit, efficiency, and the like. But leadership, properly conceived, also serves the individual human goals that our society values so highly, and we shall not achieve those goals without it.

Leaders worthy of the name, whether they are university

presidents or senators, corporation executives or newspaper editors, school superintendents or governors, contribute to the continuing definition and articulation of the most cherished values of our society. They offer, in short, moral leadership.

. . . When leaders lose their credibility or their moral authority, then the society begins to disintegrate.[11]

Another relevant quotation from the 1973 Gallup Poll on "The Public's Attitudes Toward the Public Schools," reports these data:

Are High Schools Getting Too Large?

In the 1950's James Conant argued persuasively that high schools should be large because only the large high schools could afford to have special courses in special subjects, since small high schools would not have enough students interested in these fields to warrant separate classes.

Apparently the tide has turned. Today all groups, including professional educators, are of the opinion that schools are too large; only a relatively small percentage hold that they are not big enough.

The ideal size of a school usually gets related in the typical person's mind to the size of school that he attended. To minimize this factor, a question was designed that sought to remove the issue at least one step from the respondent's own experience. The question that proved best, after testing, is as follows:

In some areas of the U.S., new towns and cities are being built. This gives city planners the opportunity to build school facilities that are "just right" in size. What do you think would be the "ideal" number of students in a high school?

After this question was asked a second question sought to elicit opinions on the general issue of whether high schools are too large or not large enough. Replies to the latter question show that major groups making up the public agree quite closely. Professional educators show even a larger proportion holding the view that schools are too large.

Here is the question:

Do you think high schools today are getting too large or aren't they large enough?

	National Totals	No Children in Schools	Public School Parents	Private School Parents	Professional Educators
	N = 1,627	928	620	124	306
	%	%	%	%	%
Getting too large	57	55	60	61	76
Not large enough	13	12	14	12	5
Just right	15	15	15	15	9
No opinion	15	18	11	12	9
	100	100	100	100	99*

(*Where sum of percentages in columns does not total 100%, it is due to rounding of the figures.)

When the views of all persons who gave a figure which represented, for them, the ideal size of a high school in a "new city," the median figure turns out to be 500.[12]

CHAPTER IX

Bibliography of Resources

CFK Ltd. Occasional Papers

Aggerbeck, Lawrence J. *A Guide to Planning School Improvements*. Englewood, Colo.: A CFK Ltd. Occasional Paper, 1973.

Brainard, Edward. *Individualizing Administrator Continuing Education*. Englewood, Colo.: A CFK Ltd. Occasional Paper, 1973.

Fox, Robert S.; Brainard, Edward; Carnie, George M.; Georgiades, William; Howard, Eugene R.; Kettering, Charles F., II; Olivero, James L. *The Principal as the School's Climate Leader: A New Role for the Principalship*. Englewood, Colo.: A CFK Ltd. Occasional Paper, 1971.

Geddes, Vivian. *Administrator Renewal: The Leadership Role and Collegial Team Development*. Englewood, Colo.: A CFK Ltd. Occasional Paper, 1973.

Houston, Clifford G., and Fox, Robert S. *An Evaluation for Individualized Continuing Education Programs for School Administrators*. Englewood, Colo.: A CFK Ltd. Occasional Paper, 1971.

Howard, Eugene R., and Jenkins, John M. *Improving Discipline in the Secondary School: A Catalogue of Alternatives to Repression*. Englewood, Colo.: A CFK Ltd. Occasional Paper, 1970.

Olivero, James L.; Geddes, Vivian; Hall, William D.; Marr, Richard E. *Self Performance Achievement Record (SPAR)*. Englewood, Colo.: A CFK Ltd. Occasional Paper, 1973.

Prince, Gerald L. *School and Self Assessment Processes: A Guidebook for Administrators*. Englewood, Colo.: A CFK Ltd. Occasional Paper, 1973.

Romine, Charles; Brainard, Edward; Petrillo, Anthony; Read, Sonya. *Learning Through Serving*. Englewood, Colo.: A CFK Ltd. Occasional Paper, 1971.

Articles, Books, and Reports

Argyris, Chris. "The CEO's Behavior: Key to Organizational Development." *Harvard Review*, March-April, 1973.

Athos, Anthony, and Coffey, Robert. *Behavior in Organizations: View*. Englewood Cliffs, N.J.: Prentice-Hall, 1968.

Bentsen, Mary M. "Study of Education Change and School Improvement: A History of the League of Cooperating Schools," *I/D/E/A Reporter*, Fall Quarter, 1969, p. 9.

Borton, Terry. "Reach, Touch, and Teach," *Saturday Review*, January, 1969, p. 56.

Brainard, Edward. "Individualizing Administrator Inservice Education." *Thrust* (Journal of the Association of California School Administrators). Vol. 2 April, 1973, pp. 29-33.

Brickell, Henry M. "The Dynamics of Educational Change," *Theory into Practice*. Vol. I, April, 1962, pp. 81-88.

Burns, T., and Stalker, G. M. *The Management of Innovation*. London: Tavistock Publications, 1961.

Cardinal Principles of Secondary Education, Bureau of Education Bulletin No. 35. Washington, D.C.: Government Printing Office, 1918.

Carnie, George M., and Prince, Gerald L. *Toward the Human Element*. 2nd ed. Vol. I. Golden, Colo.: Bell Junior High School, 1973.

Chesler, Mark; Schmuck, Richard; and Lippitt, Ronald. "The Principal's Role in Facilitating Innovation." *Theory into Practice*. Vol. 2, December, 1963. Columbus: Bureau of Educational Research and Service, College of Education, Ohio State University, pp. 269-77.

Combs, Arthur; Avila, Donald L.; and Purkey, William W. *Helping Relationships: Basic Concepts for the Helping Professions*. Boston: Allyn and Bacon, 1972.

Corrigan, R. E. *A System Approach for Education*. Garden Grove, Calif.: R. E. Corrigan Associates, 1969.

Doak, E. Dale. "Organizational Climate: Prelude to Change." *Educational Leadership*, Vol. 27, January, 1970, pp. 367-371.

Ebel, R. L., ed. *Encyclopedia of Educational Research*, 4th ed. New York: Macmillan Company, 1969, p. 1042.

Educational Policies Commission. *The Purpose of Education in American Democracy*. Washington, D.C.: National Education Association and American Association of School Administrators, 1938, p. 157.

Excerpt from *The Report of the Select Committee on Equal Educational Opportunity*. Washington, D.C.: U.S. Senate, Dec. 31, 1971. As reported to National Association of Secondary School Principals Membership in Newsletter Nov. 15, 1972, from Owen Kiernan, Executive Secretary.

Flanders, Ned A. *Teacher Influence, Pupil Attitudes and Achievement*. U.S. Department of Health, Education, and Welfare, Office of Education, Cooperative Research Project No. 397. Minneapolis: University of Minnesota, 1960.

Fleishman, E.A., and Harris, E.H. "Patterns of Leadership Behavior Related to Employee Grievance and Turnover." *Personnel Psychology*, Vol. 15 1962, pp. 43-56.

Fox, Robert S.; Lippitt, Ronald; and Schindler-Rainman, Eva. *Toward a Humane Society: Images of Potentiality*. Fairfax, Va.: Learning Resources Corp., 1973.

Fox, Robert; Lippitt, Ronald; and Schmuck, Richard. *Pupil-Teacher Adjustment and Mutual Adaptation in Creating Classroom Learning Environments*. U.S. Department of Health, Education, and Welfare, Office of Education, Cooperative Research Project No. 1167. Ann Arbor: University of Michigan, 1964 (ERIC ED-068-416).

Fox, Robert; Luszki, Margaret; and Schmuck, Richard. *Diagnosing Classroom Learning Environments*. Chicago: Science Research Associates, 1966.

Fox, Robert S.; Schmuck, Richard; Egmond, Elmer Van; Ritvo, Miriam; Jung, Charles. *Diagnosing the Professional Climate of Schools*. Fairfax, Va.: NTL Learning Resources Corp., Inc., 1973.

Gallup, George H. "Fourth Annual Gallup Poll of Public Attitudes Toward Education," *Phi Delta Kappan*, Vol. 54, September, 1972, p. 35.

Gallup, George H. "Fifth Annual Gallup Poll of Public Attitudes Toward Education," *Phi Delta Kappan*, Vol. 55, September, 1973, p. 38.

Gardner, John W. *The Antileadership Vaccine*. New York: Carnegie Corporation of New York, 1965.

Greiner, Larry, "What Managers Think of Participative Leadership." *Harvard Business Review*, March-April, 1973.

Hall, R. H. "Group Performance Under Feedback that Confounds Responses of Group Members," *Sociometry*, Vol. 20, 1956, pp. 297-305.

Harrison, Roger. "Understanding Your Organization's Character." *Harvard Business Review*, May-June, 1972.

Howard, Eugene R. "School Climate Improvement: An Essay on the Need to Humanize Our Schools." *Secondary Education Today* (Journal of the Michigan Association of Secondary School Principals). Vol. 14, Summer, 1973, pp. 36-43.

"Humanizing the Schools: Its Meaning, The Principal's Role, and Several Approaches," *NASSP Bulletin* No. 361, February, 1972.

Jackson, Phillip W. *Life in the Classrooms*. New York: Holt, Rinehart and Winston, Inc., 1968.

James, H. Thomas. "Education Dean Outlines Plans for the Future," *Stanford Review*, Vol. 19, January, 1967, p. 1.

Jung, Charles. "The Nature and Problems of Change." Chapter 2, *State Leadership in Planning and Providing for Excellence in Education*. Denver, Colo., 1971.

Jung, Charles. "Competencies for Team Leaders in Facilitating Change." *Perspectives on the Role of the Teacher Corps Team Leader*. Team Leadership Development Project, Toledo, Ohio: University of Toledo, 1971.

Jung, Charles; Pino, Rene; and Emory, R. *Research Utilizing Problem Solving: A Multi-Media Instructional System for Training Educators in Action-Research Skills*. Portland, Ore.: Northwest Regional Educational Laboratory, 1971.

Jung, Charles; Pino, Rene; and Emory, R. *Understanding Conflict and Negotiations: A Multi-Media Instructional System for Training Educators in Skills of Negotiations.* Tuxedo, N.Y.: Xicom, Inc., 1971.

Lake, Dale G.; Miles, Matthew; and Earle, Ralph B., Jr. (eds.) *Measuring Human Behavior.* New York: Teachers College Press, Teachers College, Columbia University, 1973.

Linder, Ivan H. *Characteristics of Humane Secondary School Environments.* (CFK Ltd. Commissioned Paper, 1969), pp. 2-3.

Lippitt, Ronald. "Unplanned Maintenance and Planned Change in Group Work Process." *Social Work Practice.* New York: Columbia University Press, 1962.

Lippitt, Ronald, and White, R.K. "An Experimental Study of Leadership and Group Life," in E. E. Maccoby, T. M. Newcomb, and E. L. Hartley, eds., *Readings in Social Psychology.* New York: Henry Holt, 1958.

Lippitt, Ronald; et. al. "The Teacher as Innovator, Seeker and Sharer of New Practices." In R. I. Miller, *Perspectives on Educational Change.* New York: Appleton-Century-Crofts, Inc., p. 19.

Litwin, George, and Stringer, Robert, Jr. *Motivation and Organizational Climate.* Boston, Mass.: Harvard University Press, 1968.

Lorsch, J.W. *Product Innovation and Organization.* New York: The Macmillan Company, 1965.

Mackenzie, R. Alex. *The Time Trap: Managing Your Way Out.* New York: AMACON, A Division of American Management Association, Inc., 1972.

McGregor, D. *The Human Side of Enterprise.* New York: McGraw-Hill Book Company, 1960.

Miner, John. *The School Administrator and Organizational Character.* Eugene: University of Oregon Press, 1967.

National Commission on the Reform of Secondary Education. Report of the Commission. *The Reform of Secondary Education: A Report to the Public and the Profession.* New York: McGraw-Hill Book Company, 1973.

Owens, Robert. *Organizational Behavior in Schools.* Englewood Cliffs, N.J.: Prentice-Hall, 1970.

"Perceiving, Behaving, Becoming." *The 1962 Yearbook of the Association for Supervision and Curriculum Development.*

Pino, Rene; Emory, R.; and Jung, Charles. *Preparing Educational Training Consultants: A Sequence of Four Instructional Systems for Training Educators in Skills of Consulting.* Portland, Ore.: Northwest Regional Educational Laboratory, 1971.

Resources for Social Change: A Guide for School Administrators, Vol. I, II, III. Ann Arbor: Educational Change Team, School of Education, University of Michigan, 1972.

Sargent, James. *Organizational Climate of High Schools.* Educational Research and Development Council of the Twin Cities Metropolitan Area, Inc.: University of Minnesota, 1967.

Schein, Edgar. *Organizational Psychology.* Englewood Cliffs, N.J.: Prentice-Hall, 1970.

Schmuck, Richard A., and Miles, Matthew. *Organization Development in*

Schools. Palo Alto, Calif.: National Press Books, 1971.

Schmuck, Richard A., and Nelson, Jack. *The Principal as a Convener of Organizational Problem Solving.* Center for the Advanced Study of Educational Administration. Eugene: University of Oregon, 1970.

Schmuck, Richard A., and Runkel, Philip. *Handbook of Organization Development in Schools.* Palo Alto, Calif.: National Press Books, 1972.

Schmuck, Richard A., and Runkel, Philip. *Organizational Training for a School Faculty.* Center for the Advanced Study of Educational Administration. Eugene: University of Oregon, 1970.

Schmuck, Richard A., and Schmuck, Patricia A. *Group Processes in the Classroom.* Dubuque, Iowa: William C. Brown, 1971.

Sergiovanni, Thomas, and Starest, Robert. *Emerging Patterns of Supervision.* New York: McGraw-Hill, 1971.

Silberman, Charles E. *Crisis in the Classroom: The Remaking of American Education.* New York: Random House, Inc., 1970.

Starbuck, W. H. *Organizational Growth and Development.* London: Penguin Books Ltd., 1971.

Trump, J. Lloyd, *et. al.* "Secondary Education and Human Resources." *NASSP Bulletin.* Vol. 51, May, 1967, p. 83.

Watson, Goodwin, ed. *Change in School Systems.* Washington, D.C.: National Training Laboratories, National Education Association, 1967.

Webster's International Dictionary. 2nd ed. 1938, p. 502.

Wight, Albert R. "Participative Education and the Inevitable Revolution." *Journal of Creative Behavior,* Vol. 4, No. 4, Fall, 1970.

Film

Toward the Human Element. Golden, Colo.: Bell Junior High School, 1972.

Human Resources

The educators listed below are knowledgeable about the whole area of school climate improvement, and many have provided the leadership for school based climate improvement projects. All are affiliated with CFK Ltd. as Associates and/or Program Coordinators.

Alvord Unified School District, 10365 Keller Avenue, Riverside, Calif. 92505

Eadith Atkinson, Principal, Collett Elementary School

Dr. Erwin Hollitz, Assistant Superintendent (Retired)

Dr. M. Delbert Lobb, Superintendent

Richard E. Marr, Director, School Services

Board of Cooperative Educational Services, Erie County, 455 Cayuga Drive, P. O. Box J, Buffalo, N.Y. 14225

Dr. Robert W. Sekowski, Assistant Superintendent, Instruction

Board of Cooperative Educational Services, Rockland County, 61 Parrott Road, West Nyack, N.Y. 10994

Dr. Justus A. Prentice, District Superintendent

California State University at Hayward, 25800 Hillary Street, Hayward, Calif. 94542
Dr. Lewie Burnett, Dean, School of Education

Chehalis School District No. 302, 2000 16th Street, Chehalis, Wash. 98532
Larry Norwood, Principal, Chehalis High School

Colville Public Schools, Colville, Wash. 99114
Mrs. Sharon Horstman, Teacher, Colville High School
Dr. James Monasmith, Principal, Colville High School

Compton Unified School District, 604 South Tamarind Avenue, Compton, Calif. 90220
Dr. Donald Hodes, Assistant Superintendent, Educational Services

Cuyahoga Heights Local School District, c/o 4820 East 71st Street, Cleveland, Ohio 44125
Dr. Kimball L. Howes, Principal, Cuyahoga Heights High School

Eastern Washington State College, Cheney, Wash. 99004
Dr. Jack Martin, Professor, Department of Education

East Orange Public Schools, 21 Winans Street, East Orange, N.J. 07017
Mrs. Greta D. Murchison, Executive Assistant, Office of Grants Management

Educational Service Unit No. 3, 9100 "F" Street, Omaha, Neb. 68124
Jim McDowell, Assistant Administrator

Escondido Union School District, Fifth and Maple Streets, Escondido, Calif. 92025
Ronald Brumley, Principal, Glen View Elementary School
Sidney E. Hollins, Certificated Personnel Director

Flint Hills Educational Research and Development Association, c/o School of Education, Kansas State Teachers College, Emporia, Kan. 66801
Dr. Vince Bowman, Professor

Glendale Unified School District, 411 East Wilson Avenue, Glendale, Calif. 91206
Dr. W. Roberts Pedrick, Deputy Superintendent

Idaho Falls School District No. 91, Idaho Falls, Idaho 83401
Mrs. Charleine Baum, Principal, Theresa Bunker Elementary School
Richard Bigelow, Principal, Skyline High School

Jefferson County School District, 809 Quail Street, Lakewood, Colo. 80215
Dr. George M. Carnie, Principal (now Assistant Superintendent and Co-Principal, North East Junior High School, Adams County School District 12, Northglenn, Colo.)
Gene Cosby, Area Superintendent, Golden Area
Dr. Bruce Hudson, Area Superintendent, Mountain Area
Dr. Gerald L. Prince, Counselor (now Co-Principal, North East Junior High School, Adams County School District 12, Northglenn, Colo.)

Curt Rokala, Principal, Bell Junior High School
Jerry Williams, Elementary Principal

Johnson City Central School District, 666 Reynolds Road, Johnson City, N.Y. 13790

Dr. Albert Mamary, Assistant Superintendent

Lincoln Public Schools, P. O. Box 82889, Lincoln, Neb. 68501

Dr. Elizabeth A. Dillon, Director, Staff Development
Jim Huge, Principal, Lincoln Junior-Senior High School
Vern L. Martin, Principal, Pershing Elementary School

Livermore Valley Unified School District, 71 Trevarno Road, Livermore, Calif. 94550

Dr. Justin Bardellini, Assistant Superintendent, Educational Services

Los Angeles Unified School District, 450 North Grand Avenue, Room A-307, Los Angeles, Calif. 90051

Dr. R. T. DeVries, Administrative Consultant, Staff Development Branch
Mrs. LaVerne Parks, Director, Jordan Educational Complex, Administrative Area B

Mayo High School, Independent School District 535, Rochester, Minn. 55901

Dr. Ralph E. Wright, Principal

Mesa Public Schools, 549 North Stapley Drive, Mesa, Ariz. 85203

Richard Kilbourne, Executive Director, Secondary Education

Midwest City-Del City Schools, P. O. Box 10630, Midwest City, Okla. 73110

Dr. Vernon McAllister, Director, Personnel

Mounds View Schools—District 621, 2959 North Hamline Avenue, St. Paul, Minn. 55113

Marven Rosen, Assistant Superintendent

Nebo School District, 50 South Main Street, Spanish Fork, Utah 84660

Raymond Peterson, Coordinator, Instruction

Newark Unified School District, 5715 Musick Avenue, P. O. Box 385, Newark, Calif. 94560

Dr. Donald Thomas, Superintendent (now Superintendent, Salt Lake City, Utah, Public Schools)
Mrs. Jean Weaver, Curriculum Specialist, K-6
Mrs. May Howard, Principal, John F. Kennedy School

Norwalk-La Mirada Unified School District, 12820 South Pioneer Boulevard, Norwalk, Calif. 90650

Clinton Brown, Director, Administration
Dr. Thomas E. Neel, Assistant Superintendent (now Superintendent, Ampitheater Public Schools, Tucson, Ariz.)
Dr. Louis G. Zeyen, Superintendent (now Executive Director, National Academy of School Executives, American Association of School Administrators, Arlington, Va.)

Ocean View School District, 7972 Warner Avenue, Huntington Beach, Calif. 92647

Donald Devor, Principal, Haven View School

Dr. Robert Lindstrom, Assistant Superintendent (now Assistant Superintendent, Cupertino, Calif., Unified School District)

Monte McMurray, Assistant Superintendent, Instruction

Olathe Unified School District, 1005 Pitt Street, P. O. Box 2000, Olathe, Kan. 66061

Jack Larson, Assistant Superintendent

Paradise Valley School District, 3012 East Greenway Avenue, Phoenix, Ariz. 85032

H. Ray Shipley, District Superintendent

Park County School District, P. O. Box 188, Fairplay, Colo. 80440

William R. McMillin, Jr., Superintendent

Pleasanton Joint School District, 625 Main Street, Pleasanton, Calif. 94566

Dr. William Schreck, Assistant Superintendent, Instruction

Project PSI, c/o 900 East Crest Way, Derby, Kan. 67037

Donald Crowell, Principal, El Paso Elementary School

St. Louis Public Schools, Beaumont-Sumner District, 2615 Pendleton Avenue, St. Louis, Mo. 63113

Mrs. Joan M. Bryant, Principal, Goodlach Elementary School

Benjamin M. Price, District Superintendent

San Diego City Schools, 4100 Normal Street, San Diego, Calif. 92130

Edward Fletcher, Director, Research and Development

George Montello, Elementary Principal

Dr. William H. Stegeman, Deputy Superintendent, School Operations

San Juan Unified School District, 3738 Walnut Avenue, Carmichael, Calif. 95608

Dr. Leslie M. Chase, Assistant Superintendent, Certificated Personnel

Mrs. Vivian Geddes, Curriculum Specialist

Gene Starns, Principal, Sierra Oaks Elementary School

George L. White, Principal, Bella Vista High School

School City of Gary, 620 East 10th Place, Gary, Ind. 46402

Nicholas McDonald, Director, Instruction, and District Administrator for Middle Schools

Seattle Public Schools, 815 Fourth Avenue North, Seattle, Wash. 98109

Robert Bell, Principal, Chief Sealth High School

Herbert E. Boies, Principal, Viewlands Elementary School

William D. Hall, Principal, West Seattle High School

Dr. Charles R. Hough, Director, District Relations

William Maynard, Principal, Cleveland High School

Norm Pickard, Area Administrator, South Region

Peter Schneller, Principal, Ballard High School

James Shelton, Principal, Maple Leaf Elementary School

Dr. Richard Taylor, Principal, Rainier High School

Richard J. West, Area Administrator, Region Two

Shoreline Public Schools, c/o 15345 25th Avenue, N. E., Seattle, Wash. 98155

Lynn T. Waller, Principal, Shorecrest High School

Spokane Public Schools, West 825 Trent Avenue, Spokane, Wash. 99201

Dr. Harry Finnegan, Coordinator, Program Development

Tulsa Public Schools, P. O. Box 45208, Tulsa, Okla. 74145

Dr. Gordon Cawelti, Superintendent (now Executive Secretary, Association for Supervision and Curriculum Development, Washington, D. C.)

Dr. John Dewell, Director, Staff Development

Dr. Bruce Howell, Superintendent

Unified School District 457, 211 Jones Avenue, Garden City, Kan. 67846

Dr. Horace Good, Superintendent

Dr. Jerry O. Schreiner, Director of Instruction (now Executive Secretary, United School Administration of Kansas, Topeka)

University of Utah, Department of Educational Administration, Milton Bennion Hall, Salt Lake City, Utah 84112

Dr. Lloyd E. McCleary, Professor

Ventura Unified School District, 120 East Santa Clara Street, Ventura, Calif. 93001

Dr. Patrick Rooney, Superintendent

Washington, D. C., Public Schools, c/o 2611 Moreland Place, Washington, D. C. 20015

Elmer Mitchell, Principal (Retired)

Mrs. Greta D. Murchison, Principal (now Executive Assistant, East Orange Public Schools, East Orange, N. J.)

Weber County School District, 1100 Washington Boulevard, Ogden, Utah 84404

V. E. Griffin, Assistant Principal, Roy Junior High School

Dr. Spencer Waytt, Director, Weber Community Educational Service Center

West Valley School District, c/o Route 3, Box 304 C, Yakima, Wash. 98902

William Heath, Principal, West Valley High School

Widefield School District No. 3, 701 Widefield Drive, Security, Colo. 80911

W. L. Stenson, Assistant Superintendent

Williamsville Central Schools, c/o 175 Heim Road, Williamsville, N. Y. 14221

Robert Schaefer, Principal, Heim Middle School

CFK Ltd. Foundation

Dr. B. Frank Brown, Member, CFK Ltd. Board of Directors (Director, I/D/E/A Information and Services Division, Melbourne, Fla.)

Senator George L. Brown, Member, CFK Ltd. Board of Directors (Executive

Director, Metro Denver Urban Coalition, and Member, Colorado State Senate, Denver, Colo.)

Jean S. Kettering, Chairwoman, CFK Ltd. Board of Directors, Englewood, Colo.

Leo C. McKenna, Secretary-Treasurer, CFK Ltd. Board of Directors (Vice President, Dominick & Dominick, Inc., New York, N. Y.)

Dr. Edward Brainard, President, CFK Ltd., Englewood, Colo.

Cecelia J. Logan, Executive Assistant, CFK Ltd., Englewood, Colo.

Other CFK Associates

Lawrence J. Aggerbeck, President, L. J. Aggerbeck and Associates, 376 Oakwood Court, Palatine, Ill. 60067

Dr. William E. Engbretson, President, Governors State University, Park Forest South, Ill. 60466

Dr. Robert S. Fox, Director, ERIC Clearinghouse, 855 Broadway, Boulder, Colo. 80302 (and Professor On-Leave, University of Michigan)

Dr. William Georgiades, Professor, School of Education, University of Southern California, Los Angeles

Dr. Clifford G. Houston, 3840 Armer Drive, Boulder, Colo. 80303 (Retired Professor, University of Colorado)

Eugene R. Howard, Superintendent, Urbana School District 116, 1704 East Washington Street, Urbana, Ill. 61801

Joseph J. Nold, Executive Director, Colorado OUTWARD BOUND School, P. O. Box 7247, Park Hill Station, Denver, Colo. 80207

Dr. James L. Olivero, Executive Director, Nueva Day School and Learning Center, 6565 Skyline Boulevard, Hillsborough, Calif. 94010

Grover E. Petersen, Counselor, Jefferson Senior High School, Bloomington Public Schools, 4001 West 102nd Street, Bloomington, Minn. 55431

Dr. Richard A. Schmuck, Professor, Center for Advanced Study of Educational Administration, University of Oregon, Eugene, Ore. 97403

Dr. Thomas A. Shaheen 5285 Diamond Heights Boulevard, No. 221, San Francisco, Calif. 94131 (Former Superintendent, San Francisco, Calif., Unified Schools)

Dr. Dudley Solomon, Executive Director, Children's Asthma Research Institute and Hospital, 3401 West 19th Avenue, Denver, Colo. 80204

George R. Walters, DeKalb Community Unit School District 428, DeKalb, Ill. 60115

Instruments

"Budget Simulation Game." Available from: Nueva Day School and Learning Center, 6565 Skyline Boulevard, Hillsborough, Calif. 94010

"Leadership Behavior Description Questionnaire." Available from the Bureau of Business Research, College of Commerce and Administration, Ohio State University, Columbus, Ohio 43210

"Manual for the Purdue Teacher Opinionaire," by Bentley and Rempel. Distributed by the University Book Store, 360 State Street, West Lafayette, Ind. 47906

"Organizational Climate Development Questionnaire (OCDQ)," by Andrew W. Halpin and Don B. Croft. Available from Donald B. Croft, Director, Claude C. Dove Learning Center, College of Education, New Mexico State University, Box 3AC, Las Cruces, N. M. 88001

"Personal Value Inventory," *The Launch Workbook*. Achievement Motivation Program. W. Clement and Jessie V. Stone Foundation, 111 East Wacker Drive, Suite 510, Chicago, Ill. 60601, 1972

"Personal Values vs. Institutional Values." Available from: Nueva Day School and Learning Center, 6565 Skyline Boulevard, Hillsborough, Calif. 94010, 1973

"Values Clarification," *The Launch Workbook*. Achievement Motivation Program. W. Clement and Jessie V. Stone Foundation, 111 East Wacker Drive, Suite 510, Chicago, Ill. 60601, 1972

FOOTNOTES

Preface

[1]*Webster's International Dictionary*, 2nd ed., *1938*, p. 502.

Chapter 1

[1]*Cardinal Principles of Secondary Education*, Bureau of Education Bulletin No. 35 (Washington, D. C.: Government Printing Office, 1918).

[2]Educational Policies Commission, *The Purposes of Education in American Democracy* (Washington, D. C.: National Education Association and American Association of School Administrators, 1938), p. 157.

[3]The National Commission on the Reform of Secondary Education, Report of the Commission, *The Reform of Secondary Education: A Report to the Public and the Profession* (Melbourne, Fla.: The Commission, 1973), pp. 41-46.

[4]George H. Gallup, "Fourth Annual Gallup Poll of Public Attitudes Toward Education," *Phi Delta Kappan*, Vol. 54, September, 1972, p. 35.

Chapter II

[1]R. L. Ebel (ed.), *Encyclopedia of Educational Research* (4th ed.; New York: Macmillan Company, 1969), p. 1042.

[2]H. Thomas James, "Education Dean Outlines Plans for the Future," *Stanford Review*, Vol. 19, January, 1967, p. 1.

Chapter III

[1]J. Lloyd Trump, *et. al.*, "Secondary Education and Human Resources," *NASSP Bulletin*, Vol. 51, May, 1967, p. 83.

[2]Three CFK Ltd. Occasional Papers provide precise assistance in providing these leadership services from the above list:

Reducing goals to manageable school improvement projects with measurable objectives.

Devising strategies for attaining objectives.

Evaluating progress.

Improving each project in light of the evaluative process.

These papers are:

A Guide to Planning School Improvements, by Lawrence J. Aggerbeck.

School and Self Assessment Processes: A Guidebook for Administrators, by Gerald L. Prince.

Self Performance Achievement Record (SPAR), 2nd ed., by James L. Olivero, Vivian Geddes, William D. Hall, and Richard E. Marr

Refer to Chapter IX, "CFK Ltd. Occasional Papers."

The reader is encouraged to use the material above in conjunction with this paper. The *Self Performance Achievement Record (SPAR)* is especially helpful in that it will assist the reader to directly relate self-improvement (the acquisition of needed skills, attitudes, and knowledge) to needed school climate improvement projects.

Chapter VIII

[1]Mary M. Bentsen, "Study of Education Change and School Improvement: A History of the League of Cooperating Schools," *I/D/E/A Reporter,* Fall Quarter, 1969, p. 9.

[2]U.S. Senate, Excerpt from *The Report of the Select Committee on Equal Educational Opportunity,* (1971), (As Reported to National Association of Secondary School Principals Membership in Newsletter of November 15, 1972, from Owen Kiernan, Executive Secretary).

[3]Robert S. Fox, *et al., Diagnosing Professional Climate of Schools* (Fairfax, Va.: Learning Resources Corporation, Inc., 1973), p. ix.

[4]Ivan H. Linder, *Characteristics of Humane Secondary School Environments* (Englewood, Colo.: A CFK Ltd. Commissioned Paper, 1969), pp. 2-3.

[5]Terry Borton, "Reach, Touch, and Teach," *Saturday Review,* January, 1969, p. 56.

[6]E. Dale Doak, "Organizational Climate: Prelude to Change," *Educational Leadership,* Vol. 27, January, 1970, pp. 367-71.

[7]Henry M. Brickell, "The Dynamics of Educational Change," *Theory into Practice,* Vol. 1, April, 1962, pp. 81-88.

[8]John W. Gardner, *The Antileadership Vaccine,* (New York: Carnegie Corporation of New York, 1967), p. 6.

[9]*Ibid.*

[10]*Ibid,* pp. 6-7.

[11]*Ibid.,* pp. 11-12.

[12]George H. Gallup, "Fifth Annual Gallup Poll of Public Attitudes Toward Education," *Phi Delta Kappan,* Vol. 55, September, 1973, p. 23.